Could it be that the vision has, long back, already come-
And you just didn't recognize it?
—Robert Penn Warren

The common pattern of experience, as noted before,
is always an interaction between a live creature and
some aspect of his environment, as Dewey puts it.
—Kenneth Yasuda

KATA AND THE TRANSMISSION OF KNOWLEDGE

Zen Buddist
Monk
MJE 7-00

ZEN BUDDHIST MONK

KATA AND THE TRANSMISSION OF KNOWLEDGE

IN TRADITIONAL MARTIAL ARTS

MICHAEL
ROSENBAUM

YMAA Publication Center
Wolfeboro, NH USA

YMAA Publication Center, Inc.
PO Box 480
Wolfeboro, New Hampshire, 03894
1-800-669-8892 • www.ymaa.com • info@ymaa.com

Paperback edition	Epub ebook edition
978-1-59439-026-5	978-1-59439-162-0
1-59439-026-6	1-59439-162-9

Editor: Jared Wolk
Cover design: Richard Rossiter
Cover photo: Inmagine
Illustrations by the author / enhancements by Ariana Berns

20200730

Publisher's Cataloging in Publication

Rosenbaum, Michael, -1961

Kata and the transmission of knowledge in traditional martial arts /
Michael Rosenbau. -- 1st ed. -- Boston, Mass. : YMAA Publication
Center, 2004.

p. ; cm.

Includes bibliographical references and index.
ISBN: 1-59439-026-6 (pbk.)

1.Martial arts Martial arts -- History. Military art and
science. Title.

GV1101 .R67   2004 2004114870
796.815--dc22   0410

For my wonderful wife Jen, forever and always.

And for Allan Thompson. A great fighter, but more importantly a very kind man who was always ready to help those in need. Thanks Allan for all that you did for me. I'll miss you my friend.

Contents

Acknowledgements

I wish to express my gratitude to the following people who helped during the course of writing this book. First and foremost to Mr. Ed Francisco for his insights into the role literature has played in mankind's history. Ed, your work is right up there with the great writers of our time, Faulkner, Twain, Dickey, and Harry Crews. You're a master wordsmith if there ever was one.

To Mr. Richard Lawson of Armedcombat.com. Thank you Richard your suggestions proved to be immensely valuable.

And last but not least to the staff of YMAA publishing who worked so hard on this text. Thank you, again.

What's Kata Got To Do With Anything?

> The processes of change have been so great during the
> past few decades that in many ways they threaten to
> leave us poorer instead of richer so far as our knowl-
> edge of traditional institutions is concerned.
> -Donn F. Draeger

The young man shifts gears with one hand, and steers with the other, weaving his car in and out of the rush hour traffic. On his shoulder rests a cell phone pressed tightly into his ear. "Yes Mom," he says with a sarcastic tone. "I'll be home right after class and I'll take the garbage out then." "School? What about school? Oh, it went fine today," He replies to his mother. "Just one more exam then I start preparing for the SAT." They continue talking while he downshifts, then accelerates, as if at the LeMans. The car engine whines a high-pitched squeal as the RPM's increase. Eventually the conversation ends with him promising to be home in time to finish his schoolwork, something he has been neglecting these past few months. On the radio a favorite song is being played and he turns up the volume. A heavy bass beat roars from the large speakers that are mounted where the car's back seat once was. Not only is it deafening to him but also to the people in adjacent cars. "Get a life," he laughs, as people cast hard stares in his direction, some because of his poor driving skills, others from the deafening roar that comes from the car. Down shifting into second gear, he turns into a mall parking lot. Slowly making his way over the speed bumps he finds a empty spot and parks. Getting out he grabs a gym bag and then locks the car with its remote, being careful to place his cell phone within the bag, next to his karate *gi*. Walking through the parking lot, the day's events come to mind, two early classes then back to the house for an "on-line" internet *kobudo* class. So far, it had gone well and in a couple more sessions he would have his black belt in *kobudo,* via the wonders of the world wide web. He wasn't sure if he liked the virtual reality approach better than the video black belt course he had taken last year. Both were expensive but he was learning more katas, and gaining rank in other systems, and that's what was most important. Although he had only been practicing for three years it was quite possible that by the time he turned 19 he would have black belts in two different systems and possibly six more katas through video and on-line learning. It was even possible that he might hold a master's rank by his 26th birthday.

Stopping in front of the karate school he looked up at its sign, where a samurai warrior stood in full battle dress holding a long sword in one hand and a *sai* in the other. In big gold letters was his instructor's full Anglo-Saxon name followed by "School of Bujutsu Karate-Do." His master, or *O'Sensei* as he was also called, had explained to him two years ago that this was a modern form of *bujutsu* one that had been founded on the various styles the master had studied. *Tae kwon do*, American and Okinawan karate, *ninjutsu*, several styles of Japanese sword fighting and even elements of *taijiquan* had all been woven together to form what O'Sensei had said was the most efficient martial art that had ever been created. Even though his master had only founded this system four years ago, it was still exciting to be studying a 'traditional martial art'. Inside the *dojo* he stepped onto the carpeted floor upon which sat various exercise machines and on the walls hung televisions playing the latest videos of his master performing techniques. Off to one side a student practiced one of the system's kata. Bowing in a very solemn manner, the young lady who was dressed in a bright red *gi,* slowly drew a samurai sword and assumed a ready stance. Then in quick succession, she executed three, crisp spinning heel kicks followed by a figure-eight twirling cut with the sword. Not bad, he thought, not bad at all but still room for improvement with those kicks. Looking about once more he walked towards the dressing room. In a few minutes, the kickboxercise class would end and then his sparring class would begin.

Time and Tradition. With the passing of time, our interpretation of specific rituals, traditions, rites, and even the words we speak, will differ from the custom's original implications. Take for instance the word "Spartan." When we use this word today it is done so to either describe severe conditions, or to portray someone who leads a very frugal lifestyle. However, in ancient Greece, the Spartans were one of the most respected and feared warrior societies. Theirs was a martial culture in its truest sense, a place where boys from the time of birth were trained to be warriors. It was a culture that frowned upon frivolous activities; instead it placed much value upon courage, physical prowess, and self-discipline. Today however, both our knowledge and understanding of life in ancient Greece has diminished and the traits of Spartan society with which we associate the word "Spartan" are not synonymous with the warrior culture itself. This misunderstanding also occurs with cultural traditions, especially ones that have been embedded in a society for so long that their purpose is forgotten. In such instances, cultural traditions can be considered obsolete or nothing more than folklore, when in fact their roles are vital, even if they are not recognized.

The roles that tradition plays in our lives are important. Often they are the basis for preserving our society's history and religious beliefs; and even our own identities which often rest upon long standing myths, customs, and traditions. As noted author of comparative mythology, Joseph Campbell once said, "Throughout the inhabited world, in all times and under every circumstance, the myths of man have flourished; and they have been the living inspiration of whatever else may have appeared out of the activities of the human mind and body." (Campbell, *The Hero With A Thousand Faces,* 3) A prime example of this would be the teachings of the Christian, Jewish, Buddhist, and Islamic faiths. Were it not for their long established myths, traditions, and rituals—many that are thousands of years old—it would prove almost impossible to pass religious teachings from one generation to the next.

To study the traditions of the combative arts is to understand the circumstances of their development. By understanding the process that gives birth to a system, you also gain insights into the worldviews and ethics that were prevalent during its development. The worldviews and practices of the traditional martial artist often contrast greatly to our current views and practices.

Today many people enjoy the sport of fencing but the contemporary fencer's worldviews are quite different than those of his or her seventeenth century counterpart. For modern day fencers, the idea of being killed in a 'duel of swords' is not very probable. But for those who practiced the noble art of defense some 400 years ago it was a very real and likely possibility.

The circumstances, cultural values and ethics that give rise to a combative system reach to its very core. From the weapons used, to the clothes worn by a society, they all affect a fighting arts development. Likewise the pre-arranged training routines associated with a system are also influenced by the same. In his examination of the South Indian martial art of *kalarippayattu,* Phillip B. Zarrilli said, "Because practices are not things, but an active, embodied doing, they are intersections where personal, social and cosmological experiences and realities are negotiated. To examine a practice is to examine these multiple sets or relationships and experiences. A practice is not a history, but practices always exist within and simultaneously create histories. Likewise, a practice is not a discourse, but implicit in any practice are one or more discourses and perhaps paradigms through which the practice might be reflected upon and possibly explained." (Zarrilli, *When the Body Becomes All Eyes,* 5) Zarrilli's observation is one that also proves true for pre-arranged training sequences or katas, as they are often known. Kata is a practice in which the personal, social, cosmological and realities of the age intersect and then are negotiated. Many of these early "experiences" that Mr. Zarrilli, wrote about, still influence the practice of kata and the fighting arts today. *Taijiquan* retains its identity in Daoist influences; likewise Okinawan karate has its own martial identity due to the cultural circumstances that it evolved from. This evolutionary process applies not to just a handful of fighting arts and their kata but to all styles and systems.

The basic goal of pre-arranged training is to preserve and transmit proven techniques; this remains consistent no matter what the system or style. By practicing in a repetitive manner, the fighter develops biomechanical responses that enable him or her to execute those techniques and movements in a natural reflex

JUDO

like manner. The boxer who executes a jab, uppercut, right-cross combination over and over again is trying to attain the same thing as the Okinawan karate-ka who performs *Seisan* kata ten times each day. The ultimate goal is to internalize the movements and techniques of each pre-arranged sequence (kata) so that they can be executed under almost any circumstance, without thought or hesitation. This process elucidates deeper realms of application and of learning. Donn F. Draeger wrote about the importance of pre-arranged training in relation to judo:

> Inherent in each technique of kata are "lessons" essential to an understanding of that technique, basic and variation factors, which enhance the polished performance of the technique for randori and shiai. In direct practical terms for training, this means that kata can teach the reasons why a technique will succeed or fail in randori or shiai application. However, in order to be able to find those "lessons" in the kata, the Judoka must have developed his kata out of the "doing" stage into the "using" stage.
> —(Draeger, Randori No Kata, 25)

The process of development to which Draeger refers is not one in which the kata is placed upon a pedestal for all to be admired, but instead one in which it is picked apart, technique by technique, until each one can be used by the fighter. Once this happens, the pre-arranged pattern becomes second nature. As the great Chinese writer Chuang Tzu once said,

> The fish trap exists because of the fish; once you've gotten the fish you can forget the trap. The rabbit snare exists because of the rabbit; once you've gotten the rabbit, you can forget the snare. Words exist because of meaning; once you've gotten the meaning, you can forget the words. Where can I find a man who has forgotten words so I can have a word with him?
>
> —(Chuang Tzu, 140)

Like the fish or rabbit trap, kata exists because of combat. Once its lessons were recorded and then understood, the form was set-aside so that the "meanings" Chuang Tzu wrote of would become clear.

Although "kata" is a term used often by modern martial artists to describe pre-arranged sequences of techniques, the word is a by-product of the Asian fighting arts. In actuality, the practice of combative techniques in pre-arranged forms is a methodology that has been used by many cultures throughout history, from the Roman soldier whose drills taught striking with the shield and then stabbing with his *gladius,* to modern-day karate-ka whose kata is executed so crisply in their starched white *gi.* The use of kata or pre-arranged training routines is a long standing tradition that has been employed in most fighting arts in some form or fashion. Even in those societies whose combative systems may not have been subject to the same systematic methodologies, as is found within many Asian and European fighting arts, some means were used to preserve and to transmit martial knowledge. In some cases transmission of techniques was accomplished in a highly organized manner as during the Renaissance of Europe when mathematics, the printing press, and codified techniques all came together to present a highly scientific—and at times overly analytical—analysis of the fighting arts. Yet on other occasions, the transmission of technique has been accomplished in less formal, but still eloquent means. Thomas Arnold observed about the Swiss and their martial arts that,

> This was an important development, for though the Swiss and the landsknechts certainly possessed elaborate, sophisticated and effective tactics, they apparently had almost nothing in the way of written drill. Theirs was a culture of war, not a science—it was taught by old soldier to new, and never was really codified or regularized."
> —(Arnold, *The Renaissance at War,* 64)

In each case the intent was almost the same: to preserve and pass on knowledge of battle-proven techniques, that could be used at a later date when the need warranted.[i] These routines of transmission also allowed the man-of-arms to practice certain techniques in a repetitive manner. This allowed him to perfect skills and gain artistry that made the execution of his techniques nearly as natural as walking down a city street.

Kata and pre-arranged training routines were not the only methods used to transmit and preserve martial knowledge. Dance, poetry, and written texts were used extensively to record historical events and preserve knowledge related to a society, its existence, and its martial prowess. In the early English epic *Beowulf,* the poem opens with mention of the "Spear Danes" and that "the kings who ruled them had courage and greatness." (Heaney, *Beowulf, a New Translation,* 3) *Beowulf* is not the only poetical verse that tells of a culture's martial prowess. Homer's *Iliad* is filled with passages that detail combat of the early Greek society and shows us that the development of sophisticated fighting arts by mankind is a very old practice. Dance was another medium used to practice and record martial knowledge. Both the Zulu tribes of Africa and early Filipino martial artists used dance to transmit techniques and even train warriors. The use of written text has also played an important role in spreading knowledge of the martial arts. In Europe during the Renaissance period the printing press proved to be of great value in the production and distribution of fighting arts manuals.

To study the history of kata and pre-arranged routines is to also explore methods of communication, as they went hand in hand with the practice of pre-arranged practice patterns. In fact, the same creative process that was used to develop dance, writing and poetry was also used to create kata. Just as physical shape and form is given to what were often ideals of an abstract nature, kata embodies the essence of the arts of war. It allowed man to identify, segment, practice, and then transmit concepts and techniques that otherwise would be lost in the chaotic realm of hand-to-hand combat. As Joseph Campbell said about man's ability to give physical shape to such ideas, removing them from an abstract process and thereby giving both form and meaning to the process itself, "The craft holds the artist to the world, whereas the mystic, facing inward, may be carried to such an extreme posture of indifference to the claims of phenomenal life as that of the old yogi with his parasol of grass in the Hindu exemplary tale, 'The Humbling of Indra'" (Campbell, *The Inner Reaches of Outer Space*, 89) For the fighting arts practitioner, kata or pre-arranged training routines are the bonds that holds them to this world. They are the physical manifestation of the fighting arts. Without them, and the techniques of which they are comprised, we have nothing but theory.

For the pre-modern or classical martial artist, kata practice was not just an empty routine performed for aesthetically appealing reasons. It was instead a complicated training ritual used to instill martial behavioral patterns and responses that were critical to their survival. Kata and the use of pre-arranged routines, allowed the classical martial artist to preserve techniques and behaviors that had proven successful in mortal combat. They were the "craft," that Joseph Campbell spoke of that provided the warrior with a rationalized means to examine the battlefields chaotic realm and then perfect ways to survive on it. Dr. Karl Friday said about the influence of Confucianism on Japanese martial arts and their own use of kata that:

> This infatuation is predicated on the conviction that
> man fashions the conceptual frameworks he uses to

order-and thereby comprehend-the chaos of raw experience through action and practice. One might describe, explain, or even defend one's perspectives by means of analysis and rational argument, but one cannot acquire them in this way. Ritual is stylized action, sequentially structured experience that leads those who follow it to wisdom and understanding."
—(Friday, Legacies of the Sword, 105)

The "ritual and sequentially structured experience" that Dr. Friday speaks of can be found within all methods of pre-arranged training to one degree or another.

As cultures progressed from tribal societies to city-states and then into nations, so too did their fighting arts advance in sophistication. The early Japanese were a tribal culture composed of hunters and fishermen but by the fourteenth century they had become an advanced civilization with a very sophisticated means of waging war. As the warrior increased his stature in society with his skill of arms, so did the technical aspects of his fighting arts. In keeping with this advance in "technical aspects," the sophistication of the kata and pre-arranged training patterns used within his fighting arts increased until the realms found within them went beyond the physical to include the development of his ethos and spirituality. The kata became, for not only the Japanese but also other martial cultures, a metaphor for something higher than just combative applications. It was a medium in which the spiritual and combative realms interacted as equals, two halves of a whole, that went hand-in-hand with one another, symbolic of something deeper than just a series of physical movements. It was inspired by warfare but drawn from man's creative conscious and in doing so encompassed both brutality and creativity, which stood side-by-side within his kata. Noted scholar of religious studies Karen Armstrong observed about man's creative imagination and its penchant for symbolism that,

A symbol can be defined as an object or a notion that we can perceive with our senses or grasp with our minds but in which we see something other than itself. Reason alone will not enable us to perceive the special, the universal or the eternal in a particular, temporal object. This is the task of the creative imagination, to which mystics, like artists attribute their insights."

—(Armstrong, *A History of God,* 234)

Like the mystics and artists, many warriors who performed kata began to see something of a universal nature in it. Kata became a metaphor that encompassed the duality of life and death, it reflected the transience of man and by doing so the practice became a means through which man could prepare himself for the cycle of mortality—a cycle that was often very brief for those warriors of the pre-modern era.

Pre-Modern Martial Arts. What are pre-modern martial arts? I use this term to describe those methods used extensively before firearms became the dominating force both on and off the battlefield. In categorizing man's fighting arts there are three distinct periods that can be identified, they are; *ancient, classical,* and *modern.*[ii] *Ancient fighting arts* are those that evolved when primitive man first took a stone in his hand and used it as a weapon/tool through 1400 B.C. This is the time that bronze body armor began to be worn in Mycenae cultures as well as the employment of specifically designed weapons such as the long sword, rapier, and spear. The era of the *classical fighting arts,* those systems that evolved from and ultimately took the place of the ancient methods, can be categorized between 1400 B.C. until the turn of the nineteenth century. R. Ewart Oakeshott once wrote about the sword that, "Underlying all or any tactics of battle is one basic art which for nearly 3000 years remained unchanged, in spite of chariot or war-horse, long-bow or cannon or musket—the art of hand-to-hand combat with sword and shield." (Oakeshott, *The Archaeology of Weapons Arms and Armor,* 24) And with Mr. Oakeshott's passage in mind we will define the boundaries of the classical era. Both the Ancient and Classical systems, for this book's purpose, are to be considered "pre-modern" martial arts.

With the dawn of the industrialized age and modern society's birth, many of the pre-modern martial arts were lost due to the widespread use of firearms on the battlefield. Some were preserved, while at the same time modern systems were born taking the place of those classical methods that were lost and forgotten. Just as the classical systems and their katas were intersections for the customs, personal, social and cosmological experiences of their era, so too are the *modern fighting arts* intersections for their time and place in history. Some of these modern systems maintain a linage to those classical arts before them, while others do not. Just as it was with the pre-modern systems, transmission of technique in modern methods is done through the use of kata and pre-arranged training forms. The practice of modern fighting arts and their kata however, differs greatly from those used prior to the nineteenth century. This is partly because the real threat of hand-to-hand combat no longer resonates as strongly upon the fighting arts. In examining the use of cut and thrust techniques with the sword, noted author J. Christoph Amberger presented the theory that with the sword's decline in use as an antagonistic weapon during the nineteenth and twentieth centuries, many people came to speculate about the most effective way to strike with the sword—cut or thrust? These speculations and their resulting conclusion, that the thrust was the better of the two methods, likely was not constructed in the heat of battle but from the comfort of the dining room, or in the academy under ideal circumstances where little or no danger was involved. Amberger wrote about this modern process and its lack of a realistic environment that,

> "This now commonly accepted thesis, however, has a terminal flaw: Fighters in antagonistic combat scenarios do not use definitions to dispatch each other. They use tools specifically designed for narrowly-defined purposes to achieve specific objectives against a human opponent's psyche and physiology—an opponent whose actions and motivations are often unpredictable, erratic, uncontrollable because of competing instincts, emotions, and psychological pressures."
> —(Amberger, *Hammerterz Forum*, Summer, 1997)

The same applies to modern methods of pugilism; firearms have become to our society what the sword, *naginata*, karate, kung fu and many other methods of hand-to-hand combat once were. And with the gun achieving such a dominate role in today's society, our assessments and conclusions about the conduct of hand-to-hand combat often becomes based upon theories or on the popularity of combative sports such as Judo, tournament karate, UFC etc., not the realistic environment of the battlefield, duel, or roadside ambush.

Today the circumstances, traditions and realities that brought forth the development of pre-modern martial arts systems and their training patterns are often forgotten, or reinvented such that they bear little or no resemblance to their original predecessors. When the words "kata" or "form" are spoken today quite often an image comes forth of a karate-ka dressed in a white *gi* executing crisp movements in a tournament. Yet for the pre-modern man-of-arms, his forms may have been something as simple as two or three techniques executed in a sequential pattern or performed in a more fluid but still organized manner. Systematic practice does not mean rigid; freedom of expression and application has always been a hallmark of the successful fighter. With these modern misconceptions it has become almost "en vogue" to devalue the classical martial arts. This misconception stems from the rational that these traditional methods and their "kata" have not kept up with the trends of today's fighters. There is also the argument that traditional combative systems have become obsolete due to the development of what are deemed 'new and improved' methods of hand-to-hand fighting, which supposedly serve contemporary man better than those of earlier times. With the changing face of warfare, evolution is commonplace within combative systems, but the popular belief that many of the pre-modern, or traditional martial arts, have become obsolete is often based upon a lack of understanding rather than on the fighting arts themselves. Today's full contact ring is a far cry from the battlefield upon which the medieval knight, Greek hoplite, or Japanese samurai fought and died. Such assumptions fail to consider that during the battle of

Cannae in 216 B.C. over 48,000 Roman soldiers were killed in a few hours during a battle that was conducted with sword, spear, and shield. Just one example of many such battles fought long before *modern fighting arts* came to be. The man-of-arms who fought on these early battlefields, be he Japanese samurai, Roman legion, Germanic tribesman, Mongol horseman, or many others like them, was well versed in the use of sword, spear, bow, knife and empty-handed forms of fighting. This was not an option for him but a prerequisite for his survival.

It was Socrates who said, "The unexamined life is not worth living." His statement also applies to the *modern fighting arts* and the position that kata holds within their practice. The purpose of this book is to develop an understanding of just why these rituals were used for so long in the *classical fighting arts* and just how we can benefit from them today. To do so is to study not only the history of kata training but to also explore the circumstances that gave rise to the martial arts in which they were used. It is only by understanding the process of change and evolution that affects the martial arts that we can begin to see our current practice in a clearer light and achieve a balance between past and present. To value tradition is to understand history. However, to ignore it, is to lead the "unexamined life" which Socrates spoke of, the one not worth living.

Foreword

Eastern martial arts have blossomed in the West over the past fifty years, and are practiced today for a variety of reasons including sport, civilian self-defense and even mystical fulfillment. Despite their popularity, there is little appreciation in the popular mind—and even amongst practitioners—of their origin in military and civilian forms of mortal combat, and of the existence of Western martial arts, the historical record of which is only awaiting recognition.

While it is both inevitable and wholly appropriate that the imperatives of our own age should color the practice of martial arts, our enjoyment of them can only be enriched by a better understanding of their historical origin and purpose. As a former paratrooper, a karate instructor, and a student of history, Michael Rosenbaum is well-equipped to pursue such an understanding.

Delving more deeply than the average writer on martial artists, and ranging more widely than the fragmented historical specialisms of academia, the author achieves a holistic perspective that restores martial arts to the field of military science, and shows how their development was functionally driven by the need to triumph and survive in a world much harsher than our own.

Richard Lawson
www.armed-combat.com

Richard Lawson is editor of the Internet webzine armed-combat.com, a review of military books focusing on battlefield tactics and the experience of war at the sharp end.

CHAPTER 1

Traditional Martial Arts

But their real solution was war...

—Ernle Bradford

When we use the word "traditional" today it usually denotes an Asian fighting art whose linage and teachings have been passed down from the systems founder to its present day instructors. However by using "traditional" in this manner the effect that time has on our reasons for practicing a fighting art is not recognized. *Aikido* is a traditional fighting art, but there is a vast difference between "traditional *aikido*" and the *Koryu bujutsu*, which are the "traditional martial arts" of Japan. *Aikido* is a system that was born in the early twentieth century, and although it does have combative elements within its teachings, they are very different than those found within the *Koryu bujutsu*. This is because the *Koryu* practitioners of the fifteenth and sixteenth centuries made extensive use of weaponry, wore armor, and fought on battlefields where there was uneven terrain. In contrast, today's *aikido* student practices on a level floor in a *dojo* without armor, wearing only a *gi* and *hakama*. Although both are traditional systems that were born in the same culture, *aikido* is a modern fighting art, developed in a day and age when firearms had become the dominating weapon of the battlefield. The *Koryu* by contrast are pre-modern martial arts, which were employed before firearms were the main weapons on the battlefield. Therefore the mindset, ethos, kata, and techniques of the two differ in so much as do the times in which they were developed and the manner in which warfare was conducted. Furthermore, since each system was developed in a different era, they held different roles in their respective ages.[iii] The *Koryu* were used as extensions of the state's power to further political agendas and occupy territory by means of warfare. They were designed by warriors for warriors. *Aikido*, although it does contain combative techniques, is a system used as a means for spiritual development, self-defense, and physical fitness. It was designed by civilians for civilians, and was not intended for use on the field of battle.

In defining the term "martial arts" the late Donn Draeger stated that:

> Genuine martial arts are always designed and practiced as weapons arts; any portion of training regimens devoted to "unarmed" combat is always, at the very best, secondary in nature and based, paradoxically enough, upon the use of weapons. Moreover, martial arts are primarily designed to operate on natural terrain and under any climatic conditions. Martial arts are also, carefully designed with the concept that combatants will normally wear armor, howsoever sparingly the protective devices worn may be. Another feature unique to martial arts is that they are composed of a wide range of weapons skills and do not permit specialization in a single weapon.
> —(Draeger, *Hoplos* Vol.3, No.1 Feb 1981)

Just as with our use of the word "traditional," our modern definition of martial arts differs greatly from Mr. Draeger's. More often than not when used today, the term "martial arts" is to describe Asian fighting arts like karate, *aikido*, or judo that became popular with the masses (i.e. went mainstream) during the mid to late twentieth century. Although the terms usage may be appropriate in this day and age, our modern versions are not true martial arts as Mr. Draeger described them, which were used to kill a well armed and professionally trained warrior on the battlefield. This modern usage is one that also excludes those battlefield systems used in Western societies, and others, which were as effective if not more so than their Asian counterparts. The Vikings, Celts, Egyptians, Huns, Zulus, and many other pre-modern societies had developed sophisticated and lethal martial arts systems that were used extensively to protect their societies and to take land from others.[iv] Military expansionism was very commonplace in pre-modern societies and it often proved to be an impetus for making a primitive society and its fighting arts evolve into complex warrior states with sophisticated martial arts.

The Zulus of Africa are one such example of this evolution. Prior to the nineteenth century they were cattle herders who led a very rustic lifestyle and whose battles were ritualized and considered finished when the first casualties occurred. Their weapons were made of fire-hardened wood and often were used as projectiles rather than in hand-to-hand combat. By the turn of the nineteenth century this practice had changed with encroachment on their territory from all directions. With the rise of their great warrior leader Shaka, the Zulu became a martial race in its truest sense. Shaka instituted permanent age regiments and the law that warriors could not marry until they were 40 years old. He cast aside the limitations of their ritualized warfare and designed a stabbing spear that would be used at close range. In keeping with his new weapon he also designed close-order drills and pre-arranged training patterns that taught his troops how to use the spears in combat both individually and in groups.

At its high point the Zulu nation encompassed an area of over 15,000 square miles and its leaders' methods both preserved and protected the Zulu nation. However, in the end, Shaka and his warriors succumbed to the Western ways of war. As John Keegan described him, "Shaka was a perfect Clausewitzian. He designed a military system to serve and protect a particular way of life, which it did with dramatic efficiency." (Keegan, *A History of Warfare,* 32)

Like the Zulu, the Roman Empire's territory was also maintained by its martial prowess. With a military history that dates from 753 B.C. until 554 A.D., its legions' ranks were filled with professional men-of-arms who often served for 20 years or more.[v] The Roman soldier would spend two decades of his life devoted to martial affairs and when it came to the use of his shield and sword on the battlefield, few if any could match his skills. Adrian Goldsworthy wrote of him that, "The professional Roman army was capable of defeating any of the opponents faced in late antiquity as long as it was given the resources of men and material to do so." (Goldsworthy, *Roman Warfare*, 205) The Romans and others like them were not novices to the martial arts, for 20 years of study by today's standards is what many would call a "master" and by such guidelines these early men-of-arms were masters of their craft. However, unlike the modern day counterpart, the pre-modern warriors gained much of their experience on the field of battle.

Mr. Draeger's definition of the term "martial art" is presented to establish what "pre-modern traditional martial arts" are. However this is not to discount those fighting arts like *taijiquan*, or *capoeira*, which were developed by civilians for their personal protection. This personal protection development was commonplace in pre-modern societies, and just as their battlefield counterparts did, these systems also utilized pre-arranged training patterns. Although systems such as *taijiquan*, *Okinawan te*, and other civilian fighting arts were often developed outside of the military caste, they still proved to be efficient tools for dispatching an opponent to the afterlife. Civilian fighting arts also made use of weapons; however, unlike their military counterparts the weapons used by many civilian fighting arts practitioners often were agricultural tools. Dr. Yang, Jwing-Ming discussed the use of common farming implements as weapons,

> The rake was originally designed for agricultural purposes. Farmers learned to utilize it to defend against bandits and protect their property. Farmers often trained to use all of their farming tools as weapons.

The most ancient rakes were made of wood. Later, the
head was fitted with sharp, pointed metal fingers.
—(Yang, *Ancient Chinese Weapons*, 37)

This proved true not only in Asian societies but also
European ones. The flail, hoe, and ax were used as weapons by
peasants both on and off the battlefield.

The warriors who lived and fought during the pre-modern
period were more skilled in the art of hand-to-hand combat than
we are today. This is because prior to the wide spread use of
firearms, the sword, spear, knife, crossbow, and bow and arrow
were the battlefield's premiere weapons. War was a common
event for the pre-modern warrior, and at times it was his rational, for existence. Although their praises were often sung, the
lifestyles of many of these early warriors were not easy ones.
Death came in many forms and it was not always at the hands of
your enemy. In August of 1304 A.D. the French king, Philip the
Fair, attempted to defeat a Flemish army at the battle of Mons-
en-Pevete. Heat, fatigue, and thirst took a terrible toll on the
French army, many of whom died of heatstroke and thirst in the
hot summer sun. Author Kelly DeVries said of the battle and the
French that, "They wore heavier armor than did their opponents, and they had been faced with the demoralization of constant defeat. Jean Desnouelles reports that this led to disorder
among the French army, many of whom were trying to remove
their armor to prevent heat prostration. This did not work, however, as the *Annales Gandenses* notes that many died without
being wounded, suffocating "through the weight of their armor
and the summer heat." (DeVries, *Infantry Warfare in the Early
Fourteenth Century*, 43) The brutality of pre-modern warfare was
the sounding board upon which many fighting arts were built.
Combat made the early martial arts what they were; sophisticated and efficient methods for killing an opponent on the field of
battle, for not only were personal weapons such as swords,
shields axes and crossbows used but also strategy, tactics, siege-
craft, cavalry, and even artillery. As author John Clements said
about the medieval martial arts of Europe,

> It is worth stating, though, that feudal warfare itself was not a primitive or disorganized affair by any means. It involved a good deal of documented strategy, tactics, maneuvers, and spying. Even horse archers and mercenaries were in use. As warriors, Medieval knights in particular were far from being undisciplined and rash. They prized cunning, stratagem, and prudence, but these were elusive qualities.
> —(Clements, *Medieval Swordsmanship*, 8)

These early martial arts evolved in a time when only the most effective fighting arts and techniques survived the rigors of combat. Therefore, before studying the use of training patterns, or kata, as they are often known, we should first examine the fighting arts in the ways that they were used so that we can understand the process that gave birth to both the pre-modern martial arts and their kata. Since it would be impossible to explore the development of all pre-modern fighting arts in this book, two systems, both of which were used on the battlefield, will be our examples. They are the martial arts of early Greece and the *Koryu bujutsu* of feudal Japan. Both of these systems evolved in different times, under different circumstances, and in different cultures. For the Japanese the epitome of their martial prowess was the *Bushi* or samurai, a member of the aristocratic warrior class, who ruled Japan in a totalitarian manner. As S.R. Turnbull said about them and their rise to power,

> It would be misleading to see the rise of the samurai as a democratic movement, which the picture of brave farmers uniting behind a champion to defend their interests, may suggest. With few exceptions, the powerful landowner who was the nucleus round whom the military force gathered, was of noble, and often royal blood. It is interesting to note that, in the provinces, although military prowess was a test of leadership, an aristocratic pedigree was a definite asset in attracting support. As this support grew, so did the sense of identity based on a newly established idea of the clan. The clans of the pre-Reform era, which the land reforms had set out to abolish, reappeared as the samurai clans.
> —(Turnbull, *The Samurai, A Military History*, 16)

In contrast to the samurai, the Greek martial arts evolved from systems that were used exclusively by the aristocratic warrior class of the Mycenaean era into those used by the hoplite of classical Greece, whose trademark was a very cohesive formation called the phalanx. Like the samurai the Greek martial arts evolved from the society that used them. The Classical Greeks were not ruled by a military elite but rather by democratic process, as such every man was considered a warrior to whom fell the duty of defending his land and loved ones. To quote William Durant, "The Army is identical with the electorate; every citizen must serve, and is subject, until the age of sixty, to conscription in any war." (Durant, *Life of Greece*, 264) Although often considered simplistic, the Greek martial arts were a complex and sophisticated means of fighting, which employed the use of both armed and unarmed methods of combat and embraced its own distinctive warrior ethos. It honored courage and tenacity on the battlefield as is shown in Plato's *Laws* which stated that,

> A man who is stripped of his shield by a considerable exertion of force cannot be said to have flung it away with the same truth as one who drops it of his own act. There is all the difference in the world between the cases. So, we shall give our law this wording. If a man surrounded by the enemy, and having arms in his hands, do not turn to try and defend himself but intentionally throw down his weapons, or cast them away, and thus chose to purchase a life of shame by his cowardice rather than fair and glorious death by his valor, there shall be judgment for the loss of arms flung away; in the other case above mentioned, the judge will hold careful inquiry.
> —(Plato, *Collected Dialogues, Laws XII* 944C)

Even though they evolved at different times in history, their skill of arms was a necessity for both the samurai and the hoplite, not only for their survival but also for the survival of their societies. Death in battle was an accepted fate by these men-of-arms, and at times they even relished the idea because of the tribute paid to those who had fallen in battle by their respective cultures. Neither the samurai nor the hoplite suffered from that most dangerous tendency that Herodotus spoke of, "a wish to kill but not to die in the process." (Hanson, *Western Way of War*, 10) This is very evident by the manner in which both preferred to do battle—at close range. For those of their ranks who did shun their duty on the battlefield, the shame and dishonor cast upon them often proved more painful than the sentence of death they had run from.

1-1 THE GREEK MARTIAL ARTS

> Two Medes lunged toward the Spartan with lances leveled, only to be intercepted by the massive bowl of his rankmate's shield, dropping into place to defend him. Both enemy lances snapped as their heads drove against the bronze facing and oak bowl work of the shield. In the rush, their momentum carried them forward, sprawling onto the ground atop and tangled with the first Spartan. He drove his xiphos into the first Mede's belly, rose with a cry of homicide and slashed the second hilt-deep across both eyes. The enemy clutched his face in horror, blood gushing between the fingers of his clenched and clawing hands. The Spartan seized with both hands his own fallen shield and brought its rim down like an onion chopper, with such force upon the enemy's throat that it nearly decapitated him.
>
> —(Pressfield, *Gates of Fire*, 259)

Gates of Fire is Steven Pressfield's splendidly written book about the battle of Thermopylae and a small group of Spartans who went knowingly to their death so that other Greeks could build defenses against the onslaught of Xerxes' Persian army. Despite their bravery at Thermopylae, the Spartan's tenacity and skill of arms was recognized throughout Greece long before the battle was ever fought. The Spartans, however, were just one group of people who made up a highly advanced civilization that had a long and illustrious martial heritage.

Greece was an agrarian society of city-states. This was a society in which the same language was spoken and even the same customs and traditions were observed—a culture from which came such great minds as Socrates, Plato, and Aristotle. War was a integral part of their society; it was a crucible where mans best and worst traits were revealed and it gave life to much of what the Greeks valued in their world. Their literature, philosophy—even their plays were all inspired by the field of battle. Victor Davis Hanson said of them that; "The soldier and the farmer may be forgotten or even despised in our own culture, but in the Greek mind agriculture and warfare were central to a workable society, in which both professions were to be controlled by a rational and egalitarian citizenry." (Hanson, *The Wars of the Ancient Greeks* 18) As early as 3000 B.C. there were both society and culture in Greece. However it wasn't until the Bronze Age that stone buildings, fortresses and cities begin to appear. The Minoans built the first of these on the island of Crete. Despite the fact that they didn't speak Greek they still exerted strong influences on the rest of early Greek culture.

The Minoan culture advanced rapidly, and by 2000 B.C. they had begun constructing large palaces that served the population's social, governmental, religious and administrative needs. They were an advanced society with skilled navigators who traded with Egypt and other cultures. They also loved their combative sports. Will Durant said of them that,

> In the towns he patronizes pugilists, and on his vases and reliefs he represents for us a variety of contests in which lightweights spar with bare hands and kicking feet, middleweights with plumed helmets batter each other manfully, and heavyweights, coddled with helmets, cheekpieces, and long padded gloves, fight till one falls exhausted to the ground and the other stands above him in conscious grandeur.
> —(Durant, *The Life of Greece*, 12)

The demise of Crete's Minoan culture is attributed to several events. Some historians believe it is because of the trade with Egypt being disrupted after Ikahanton's death while others credit it to the eruption of a volcano located on a small island north of Crete. Whichever disaster it was, if in fact not both, the Minoans never fully recovered and before long they were conquered by their aggressive and resourceful neighbors. Around 1400 B.C. Mycenaean forces invaded and occupied Crete and for the next 200 years controlled much of the Aegean area.

The Mycenaeans of 1600 to 1100 B.C. spoke a language very similar to later day Greeks and inhabited the southern Greek mainland. The exact date of their forefathers arrival in Greece is unknown but many speculate that it was somewhere between 2100-1600 B.C. They were skilled metalsmiths who captured the Aegean marketplaces with their arts and crafts. Their methods of warfare were conducted much the same as the earlier Egyptians with chariot, javelin-throwers, bow and arrow, and missile-men. The chariot itself was a formidable weapon and gave a high degree of maneuverability to warriors in a day and age when fighting on foot was commonplace. It also allowed its occupants to circle their opponents from a distance and either toss javelins or shoot at them with bows and arrows. The results could prove devastating and often did. Historian John Keegan observed about the use of the chariot in ancient societies that;

> Ten minutes work by ten chariots would cause 500 casualties or more, a Battle of the Somme-like toll among the small armies of the period. In the face of such an attack by which it could not maneuver out of trouble, the stricken host had only two choices: to break and run or to surrender. In either case, the outcome for the charioteers would have been a large booty in prisoners, probably rapidly destined to become chattel slaves.
> —(Keegan, *A History of Warfare,* 166)

Although its use in mass formations was limited by the rugged terrain of Greece, chariots nonetheless were prized weapons as Homer's *Iliad* shows when the wise old warrior Nestor, leader of the Greeks from Pylos, briefs his troops before battle:[vi]

> Nestor positioned the chariots in front
> And massed the best foot soldiers at the rear
> Within this double wall he stationed riffraff, 320
> So that willing or not they would be forced to fight.
> Nestor briefed his charioteers first,
> reminding them to control their horses

And not drive recklessly into the melee:
"Now don't get overconfident, any of you,
Or be to eager to fight the Trojans alone,
In front of the rest. But no falling back either.
Either course will weaken the line.
When you make contact with an enemy chariot,
Stay in your own and thrust with your spear." 330
—(Homer, *Iliad*, 74)

In addition to being used to break up the ranks of enemy foot soldiers, the chariot also served to carry warrior chieftains to the battlefield where they would dismount and then fight on foot. Carrying their spears in hand, they would throw them at their enemies from a distance. If not successful they would then toss heavy stones at one another, closing distance until swords could be used. (Warry, *Warfare in the Classical World*, 15) This method was a far cry from those of later day Greeks who utilized the phalanx.

During the renaissance of martial arts in later day Europe, numerous manuscripts were printed that described the technical details of their fighting arts. This was not so in Mycenaean culture because reading and writing were skills known only to a small percentage of the population. Written communications of the Mycenaean culture were done in the form of Linear B,

EARLY MYCENAEAN RAPIER FROM AROUND 1500 B.C. ITS BLADE WAS HEAVIER AND BROADER THAN OTHER CULTURES' VERSIONS DEVELOPED AROUND THIS TIME. THE WEAPON COULD ALSO BE USED TO CUT, ALTHOUGH IT WAS MOST EFFECTIVE WHEN USED FOR THRUSTING.

which consisted of a syllabary of some 90 logograms. It was used primarily to record palace accounts of sheep, flax, wheat, and even chariots. Linear B was not used for narrative prose. As Jared Diamond said about its use, "Linear B was inherently so ambiguous that it remained restricted to palace accounts, whose context and limited word choices made the interpretation clear. Not a trace of its use for literature has survived." (Diamond, *Guns, Germs, and Steel,* 235) Because there is no written account of the Mycenaeans having a codified martial art does not mean that one didn't exist. The weapons of this era prove otherwise, as does the emphasis placed on the skill of individual warriors.

There were three distinct periods of weapons development in the Mycenaean Culture; the Shaft-Grave Period, the Palace Period, and the Late Period. (Snodgrass, *Arms & Armor of the Greeks,* 15-27) Excavations from the Shaft-Grave period have unearthed large spearheads and short swords, which could be used for slashing strokes and cutting. However, one of the most interesting weapons found from this era are long rapiers that measured three feet in length and more.

The manufacturing of body armor at this time in Mycenaean culture did not employ the same methods as later day Greece. Much of the body armor worn was made of cowhide; therefore a thrusting weapon could penetrate it. A rapier is a thrusting weapon, and the thrust itself is a technique, that has to be learned. To quote A.M. Snodgrass who said about the use of these large swords, "Strictly these are thrusting weapons, and their designed use must have been largely limited to the fencing duels, between single champions, which we see represented on some signet-rings of the period." (Ibid., 16) The ancient rapier's development is due in part to the use of daggers by early man, and the lengthening of their blades through constant sharpening and metal-smithing techniques. However, when one develops a weapon they inadvertently give birth to its systematic use. It was by the very nature of these weapons that the Mycenaeans gave birth to established techniques and in time, training patterns for their warriors to further perfect their skills. To design a rapier for use in battle is to also design a fighting art. Each weapon has its own characteristics and the movements and techniques associated with the rapier differ from those used with cut-and-slash weapons. In the development of a thrusting weapon like the rapier the early Greeks also came to recognize the dangers inherent to puncture wounds. A cutting or slashing stroke that is often used against heavily armored opponents will not prove immediately fatal unless it severs a limb or artery. If the wounded warrior receives medical attention after the wound has been inflicted, there is a chance for survival; however, a puncture wound that penetrates the lungs, abdomen, heart, eyes, or kidneys will prove fatal despite the care given, and since much of the armor worn at this time could be penetrated by a rapier, the weapon proved effective on the battlefield. Addressing the use of the rapier in Renaissance times John Clements provides insight into the weapon's effectiveness when he discussed its use and the wounds inflicted,

> As a thrusting sword, the rapier took advantage of all this. By putting emphasis on thrusting kills (for effi-ciency and speed), one naturally finds oneself point-ing the blade at the opponent. This is one of the main differences between a rapier and a cut-and-thrust sword. The "on-guard" position is point-on and not with the weapon held back, angled high or tip raised. Fighting point-versus-point necessitates blocking the attacking thrust while countering your own. Rapier techniques inherently use counterattacks in the man-ner of simultaneously preparing for (thrust) attacks as parries are made (a concept familiar in Japanese sword arts). Its ability to riposte (counterattack) can be quick and effective.
> —(Clements, *Renaissance Swordsmanship*, 9)

To fight with a rapier against another armed opponent requires some skill and training. It is not a task that should be undertaken by the novice. With a lack of written information about the Mycenaeans' rapier skills, it would be hard to deter-mine if they were as advanced as those of the European renais-sance martial artists some 3,000 years later. Many scholars doubt that the Mycenaeans' rapier skills evolved to high levels of prac-tice. However, it is possible that the practice of the sword did progress to substantial levels of expertise in early Greek society, but by the classical era many people had come to believe that the art of swordsmanship served little purpose on the battlefield. In the "Dialogue between Laches, Nicias, Lysimachus, and Socrates," the merits of swordsmanship on the battlefield are dis-cussed. Since all of the participants in the discussion had distin-

guished themselves in combat, and both Laches and Nicias were generals, the common view held about the art of swordsmanship; it serves well as a form of entertainment but there is little use for it on the fields of slaughter where the hoplite plied his trade. Laches observes about those who publicly exhibit the art of swordsmanship that,

> I have encountered a good many of these gentlemen in actual service, and have taken their measure, which I can give you at once, for none of these masters of fence have ever been distinguished in war—there has been a sort of fatality about them; while in all other arts the men of note have been always those who have practiced the art, these appear to be a most unfortunate exception.
>
> —(Plato, *Collected Dialogues*, 127)

One possible reason for his dim view on swordplay is that by this time in Greek warfare, the phalanx had made those individual duels, conducted by the Myceanean warriors, obsolete. No one man could hope to stand and prevail against the hoplites massed ranks. The sword was still a deadly weapon; however, its role on the battlefield was considered secondary at this time in Greek history.

Following the Shaft Grave period came the Palace and Late periods of Mycenaean history. In the Palace era advances in bronze-smith techniques allowed body armor to be produced and worn. In terms of weapons, new ones were designed that allowed for cutting strokes. In addition to new swords, larger spearheads were also developed that allowed for more effective thrusting and slashing action. Archery was also practiced and archers were used in both formations and from chariots.

In the late period of Mycenaean history, 1300 B.C., migra-tions into the Aegean by Hellenic speaking marauders fr[om] north brought changes in both weapons and tactics. [These] marauders were a highly mobile people who could strike al[most] anywhere without warning due to their seafaring skills. They [also] fought on foot, as cohesive formations, without the aid of hea[vy] bronze armor, chariots, archers, or horses. With these outsi[de]

The methods [...]
neatly within the IHS [...]
Greek hoplite and his skill of [...]
like the *Koryu bujutsu* of Japan in w[...]
the hands and feet, attacking vital areas, the [...]
armor were all used. In defining what a combat [...]
IHS goes on to explain the categories of use for a co[...]
tem. They are:

Mortal

  1. Battlefield mortal combat
    a. battlefield single combat
    b. battlefield group combat
  2. Civil self-defense
    a. group self-defense
    b. single self-defense
  3. Duel

Non-Mortal

  4. Agonistic-sport or other types of ath[letic]
    competition.
  5. Psychological-usually evolved from [...]
    now applied toward religious-philos[ophical]
    concepts and goals. (Armstrong, Hop[...]

PANKRATIASTS

The Greek martial arts are primarily battlefield systems designed for group combat, or to use the IHS's definition they are, "1. battlefield mortal combat, b. battlefield group combat" systems. However this is not to say that their sole function was for group combat because the hoplite's skill could and was used on an individual basis. Likewise their fighting arts were not just limited to the the battlefield for their combative sports encompassed not only wrestling, but also boxing, stick fighting—which was useful in developing sword and spear skills—and *pankration,* a sport that allowed the fighters to not only box and wrestle but kick as well. In all of their combative sports, contests were held outdoors in the hot summer sun, where pugilists fought naked and with no time limits. Gouges to the eyes, kicks to the groin, and strangulation techniques were all used by the Greek fighters. Michael B. Poliakoff described *pankration* and the dangers involved with it best when he said,

> Pankration was a heated contest, and the competitor had to be prepared for considerable discomfort-kicks, punches, sand in the mouth, wrenched limbs, choke-holds. In addition to Arrichion, we learn from an

inscription of another pankratiast who died in the contest, and the trainer of one pankratiast is said to have written to the athlete's mother, "If you should hear that your son has died, believe it, but if you hear he has been defeated, do not believe it."
—(Poliakoff, *Combat Sports in the Ancient World*, 63)

The skills developed by the Greeks in their combative systems, both for sport and the battlefield, were not haphazardly imparted. They were taught in an organized manner, which involved much physical conditioning and the utilization of pre-arranged training patterns. In Plato's *Laws* the Athenian and Clinas discuss society and its governing laws, both good and bad, when their conversation turns to the training of boxers. As they walk along discussing the issues at hand the Athenian states the following,

Well, then, suppose our training were meant for boxers, or pugilist, or athletes in some similar competition. Should we be for going straight into the actual contest without any previous daily combat with an opponent? Surely, were we boxers, for days together before the actual event we should be learning how to fight and working ourselves hard. We should rehearse all the movements we expected to make in the actual match, when the time for it should come, and we should come as near as we could to the reality; we should fit our hands with practice gloves in place of match gloves, to make sure that we were getting the best training we could."
—(Plato, *Collected Dialogues, Laws III* 830 A-B)

His statement indicates that their fighting arts were practiced in pre-arranged methods. Skimachia, or shadow boxing, was also very popular among the Greeks and is often known as "free form" in Asian fighting arts circles. The systematic training that the Athenian and Clinas talk of was also found within their battlefield martial arts. Many have pointed to the Greeks and declared that their methods were effective, yet required little or no training and were performed by novices. Many of the hoplites were part-time soldiers and full-time farmers but other cultures with sophisticated martial arts have done so as well. J. Christoph Amberger said about the attitude held by many towards the Greeks and their fighting arts;

> To them, Greek armies are accumulations of armed amateurs with little or no training. But they forget that armed amateurs were also the mainstay of European martial arts for over 1,000 years. Both the Masters of Defence in London and the Central European fighting guilds consisted of urban professionals and craftsmen—who spent every spare minute practicing the weapons and systems of their avocation."
>
> —(Amberger, *Hammerterz Forum*
> Spring/Summer 1996)

Likewise Socrates gives us indication that the hoplites' skill of arms was practiced and perfected on an individual basis when he said about the two brothers Euthydemus and Dionysodorus that,

> I never knew till now what all-round athletes were! These two are quite all-champions! They surpass the two Acarnanian brothers, those all round athletes, for those could do nothing but fight with their bodies. But these! First of all they are first-rate in fighting with their bodies and battling with all comers—they are themselves masters at fighting in armor, and can make anyone else expert who would pay their fee.
>
> —(Plato, *Euthydemus* 271C, 386)

To some, the Greek martial arts may seem simple, but in combat, simplistic often means success. Just as the pankrationist, the hoplite also used prearranged forms to perfect his skills. The Greek war dance known as "Pyrrhic" included included striking with a spear, eluding blows, body shifting, and intricate footwork, Plato wrote, "it depicts the motions of leaping from the ground or crouching as well as contrary motions which lead to a posture of attack." (Plato, *Laws VII*, 815) The hoplite was many things, but he was not an amateur when it came to the art of war.

It was the role played by agriculture and war in Greek culture that gave birth to the hoplite. By the year 700 B.C. Greece had emerged from its dark ages into a society where individuals owned property—farmers had created an agricultural community that extended far beyond the reach of city walls. In the midst of this new era, advances were being made in metallurgy, writing, arts, and philosophy. It was the birth of what could be considered a middle class society, one from which the hoplite and his phalanx was born. Since many of these early Greek agricultural communities had no fortifications, the idea of warfare conducted in the open was adopted. It was reasoned that the largest group of men should be mustered and meet their enemies in one tumultuous clash that would end the conflict in a few short hours of bloodshed, instead of having a prolonged engagement that would disrupt farming, and destroy valuable land and crops.

A culmination of forces resulted in the birth of the hoplite and his phalanx. One was advances in metallurgy, which allowed for better armor and weapons to be manufactured by the Greeks. Unlike their Mycenaean ancestors who wore either cowhide or ill-fitting bronze plate, the Greeks of the Classical period were able to develop bronze corsets and helmets that protected both their heads and chests. It also allowed for the making of a round shield made from bronze and iron called the *hoplon* that weighed anywhere from 17-25 pounds. It is from the shield that the hoplite gained his name. (Hanson, *Western Way of War*, 26) Their arms consisted of an eight-foot spear that was used in one hand while the hoplite held his shield with the other. In addition to his spear he also carried a small sword called a *kopis*. This was a secondary weapon, which was used at close quarters when the ranks of the phalanx had begun to separate. The *kopis* was an extremely effective slash-and-cut weapon because of its curved blade. Forerunner of the Gurkha's *kukri*, the *kopis,* if used by an experienced person, could slice off an opponent's arm or leg. All told, the hoplites' arms and armor could weigh almost 70 pounds, which is an amazing amount of weight for a warrior while fighting hand-to-hand and on broken ground.[viii]

The mindset and social values of Classical Greece had as much to do with the hoplites' birth and the Greek way of war as their weapons did. Theirs was a society in which citizen militias

THE PHALANX

were valued more than an aristocratic elite warrior. It was also a society in which the individual's ideas and political expressions were welcomed in public debates. Theirs was the forerunner of a modern day democracy and it was their collective mindset that gave birth to the Greeks' way of war. The phalanx reflected the Greek society from which it came. It was a formation in which all members of a community or town served side-by-side, where they shared both victory and death. The size of the formation itself varied with the number of hoplites within it. Some were eight men across and up to twelve men deep. The hoplites stood shoulder to shoulder so that their shields could afford them the most protection. The rows behind stood with their shields pressed against the back of the man in front. Armed with their eight-foot spears, only the first three ranks could employ their weapons, those hoplites behind ended up pushing those in front so that there was always a continuous forward motion.

The phalanx was a fierce sight to behold. hoplites dressed in armor, helmets covering their faces except for small slits from which to see, massed in a tight formation, from which long spears thrust forward to kill or maim any foe in their path. They took to the battlefield in a stoic manner, and then marched forward as a whole entity whose sole purpose was to slaughter its enemy. In *The March Up Country*, Xenophon recounts the reaction of the

Cilician queen who begged for a display of the Greek's martial prowess. Adorned in all of her finery, she sat upon a carriage with her servants waiting for the phalanx to march towards her. Xenophon recounts that,

> The captains passed on the order to the men; and when the trumpet sounded they presented pikes and advanced. Then the pace quickened. The men doubled towards the tents with cheers of their own accord. There was a panic among the national troops, and the Cilician fled in her wagon, and the people from the market fled too, leaving their goods behind. The Cilician was amazed to see the brilliancy and discipline of the army; and Cyros was delighted when he saw how the natives were scared by the Hellenes.
> —(Xenophon, *March Up Country*, 6)

The phalanx was the Greeks "craft" that Joseph Campbell spoke of, which bound them to this earth in terms of warfare. It was a very pragmatic yet ritualized tradition that allowed them to segment, study and then train themselves for war. Earlier in his book Dr. Karl Friday was quoted as saying: "Ritual is stylized action, sequentially structured experience that leads those who follow it to wisdom and understanding." (Friday, *Legacies of the Sword*, 105) His statement certainly proves true for the Greeks because the phalanx was, as he put it, a "sequentially structured experience," which spurred forth much wisdom and understanding about the art of war.

In his book *The Western Way of War*, Victor Davis Hanson describes six phases of phalanx combat. They are:

- The Need to Move Forward
- The Run In
- No Man's Land
- The Collision
- Tears and Gaps
- The Push and Collapse

Phase 1—The Need to Move Forward occurred when the Greeks drew up their battle lines. Combat was a formalized affair in which ambushes, unexpected attacks, and other actions of this nature were generally frowned upon but not ruled out completely. The two sides would meet at an appointed place where they would draw their battle lines and stand eyeing each other across the field of battle. The option given to the hoplite was quite clear; he had only one and that was to charge forward into the sharp spears of his enemy. When the order was given the phalanx moved forward towards the enemy, and it was at this point that the hoplites' training came into play. For those like the Spartans, whose society trained constantly for war, the cohesion of the formation would be maintained. However, for others who trained infrequently, it was soon lost.

Phase 2—The Run In. After the phalanx had started their advance, and at a set distance from the enemy, the hoplites began to run forward. This was done to build forward momentum and to increase the shock of their attack. The loss of forward movement could only mean one thing and that was that the front ranks had faltered and defeat was soon at hand. It was at this point in the advance where fear and exhaustion from movement could cause the phalanx's ranks to become disordered. Because of the heavy bronze armor worn, the order to run if too far from the enemy would result in an exhausted hoplite, especially if the attack was executed during the summer. Fear also played a major role, as those in the first three ranks tried to cover themselves with their shields prior to colliding with the enemy's own phalanx. As Thucydides said about the experience,

> It is true of all armies that, when they are moving into action, the right wing tends to get unduly extended and each side overlaps the enemy's left with its own right. This is because fear makes every man want to do his best to find protection for his unarmed side in the shield of the man next to him on the right thinking that the more closely the shields are locked together, the safer he will be. The fault comes originally from the man on the extreme right of the front line, who is

> always trying to keep his own unarmed side away
> from the enemy, and his fear spreads to the others
> who follow his example."
>
> —(Thucydides, *History of the*
> *Peloponnesian War*, 392-393)

Phase 3—No Man's Land. When the charge is well under-way the formation advances almost at a run, sweat pours from beneath the hoplite's armor and breathing is heavy, dust clouds rolling from the movement of so many men clog his vision. Only those in the front three ranks have any sense of how close they are to the enemy. The hoplite's hearing is impaired not only because of his helmet, but from the noise of clanging equipment and the shouts of those around him. He feels almost suffocated from the heat and proximity of the hoplites who surround him. Within, he knows that the two forces are about to meet in a deadly headlong collision.

Phases 4-6—Collision, Tear and Gaps, Push and Collapse. When the ranks collided the hoplite's sense of perception would become smaller, often to just the man in front and the man to each side of him. He finds himself entangled in a mass of human bodies, that are killing one another with spear thrusts to the groin, neck, face, and chest. Those spearmen of the second and third ranks extended their weapons over the shoulders of those in front so that the phalanx becomes an entity of its own, killing and maiming any who stand before it. Steven Pressfield best described the phalanx's collision through the eyes of a young Spartan when he wrote: "I had never appreciated how far beyond the interleaved bronze of the promachoi's shield the murderous iron of their eight-footers could extend. These punched and struck, overhand, driven by the full force of the right arm and shoulder, across the upper rim of the shield; not just the spears of the front-rankers but those of the second and even third, extending over their mates shoulders to form a thrashing engine that advanced like a wall of murder." (Pressfield, *Gates of Fire*, 106) For the men in the front ranks it was pure murder, chaos reigned, but their training and instincts took over. Those without spears would use their deadly *kopis*; this stage of close quarter combat occurred quickly in the front ranks due to the proximity of the combatants and the force at which they collided causing many of their spears to break. Both sides would be intermingled with one another slashing and hacking with their *kopis* while other hoplites continued to gouge into the tangled mass of bodies with their spears. Along with their boxing and wrestling skills,[ix] the entire spectrum of the Greek combative arts was utilized in that hell on earth where the two phalanxes collided and the hoplites butchered one another, hand to hand, face to face.

To those hoplites in the rear ranks fell the job to constantly push forward, their spears pointed skyward to deflect incoming arrows and also dispatch any enemy wounded with a downward jab of the spear butt. (Hanson, *The Wars of the Ancient Greeks*, 172) If a stalemate occurred it was their job to end it by exerting a steady push and to keep anyone from turning back. Often men were trampled to death after the initial collision because they had fallen, then were unable to get up from the mass of human bodies that stood over and on them. The fighting lasted until one side could no longer stand the bloodshed, too large a number killed or wounded, being out flanked, loss of nerve and courage, or all of the above. When this happened, a rout usually occurred and many would flee from the battlefield. As for the wounded, there were two categories: those injured slightly and those severely wounded by a thrust to the abdomen, groin, back, chest or elsewhere. For these hoplites the chances of survival was slim if any. If they did not die in battle, it was almost assured that they would die later from infection.

Within Western society war has been considered acceptable under two conditions: that it be of either a holy nature or for a just cause. Holy wars, like the Christian crusades, are fought because of a society's theocratic views, and are sanctioned by a divine authority, like the pope, or in Joshua's case, being commanded by God to war against the Ai people:

> "And the Lord said to Joshua, Fear not, neither be dismayed: take all the men of war with you, and arise and go up to Ai; because I have delivered into your hands the king of Ai and his people, his city his land;

SPARTAN WARRIOR

2 And you shall do to Ai and its king as you did to Jericho and its king; only the spoil and the cattle shall you take as a prey for yourselves; lay an ambush against the city,from behind it   —Joshua 8."

Joshua did as the Lord commanded, he destroyed the city and killed 12,000 men and women during the course of his campaign.
—(Russell, *The Just War*, 9)

Just wars are those waged for non theocratic reasons, such as defense from invaders, prevention from being conquered and enslaved, prevention of genocide, etc. In such cases, those fighting for their lives considered any means available fair. For the Greeks, war was a natural occurrence among its city states. War was considered just and was conducted in a structured manner. The Greeks viewed the battlefield as something essential to the ethos of their society. Plato stated when it concerned war among the Greeks; "In my opinion, just as we have the two terms, war and faction, so there are also two things, distinguished by two differentiae. The two things I mean are the friendly and kindred on the one hand and the alien and foreign on the other. Now the term employed for the hostility of the friendly is faction, and that of the alien is war." (Plato, *Collected Dialogues*, 70) Plato's comment gives much insight into how when the Greeks fought one another, it was a just war waged in a fair manner, if there is such a thing to be found on the battlefield. However, when it came to waging war against those from outside of Greece—against the barbarians as Aristotle considered them—the Greeks were anything but just and fair on the battlefield.[x]

Thermopylae.
Go tell the Spartans, you who read:
We took their orders, and are dead.
—Spartan epitaph for those killed
in the battle of Thermopylae

The warriors of Thermopylae have, for 2,500 years of western civilization, exemplified the traits a warrior should exhibit. discipline, self-sacrifice to a cause greater than oneself, honor, courage, and martial prowess. For the Spartans who died at Thermopylae their skill of arms, and ultimate death was a source of honor in their society. Those who marched off to that infamous field of battle knew before hand that the likelihood of their returning alive was slim , if in fact it was even considered by any of them. The discipline, skill of arms, and mindset of the Spartans was equal to those of later day Japanese samurai; the army was the moral nucleus of their society. To be a warrior was to embody all that was held sacred—courage, strength, and martial prowess. These traits were the pride of the Spartans. William Durant said of them that, "Around this army Sparta formed its moral code: to be good was to be strong and brave; to die in battle was the highest honor and happiness; to survive defeat was a disgrace that even the soldier's mother could hardly forgive. "Return with your shield or on it," was the Spartan mother's farewell to her soldier son. Flight with the heavy shield was impossible." (Durant, *The Life of Greece,* 81) For the men of Xerxes' army, who fought at Thermopylae and lived to tell the tale, they did not give much thought to the Spartans' moral code, but they never overcame the terror of those three days during which they witnessed a handful of Spartans, along with their Thespian, Theban and Helot allies, kill close to 20,000 of their number. Of particular distress to the Persians was the Spartans' nonchalant attitude towards battle: seeming as if not only were they seeking combat but that they sought out death as well. They marched into battle as if on the parade ground and killed with a precision and dispassion never seen before by Xerxes' men.

Xerxes' invasion of Greece in 481 B.C. was the continuation of his father's failed attempt ten years before which met with disaster at Marathon. There a force of 11,000 Greek hoplites defeated a Persian army three times their size within a few hours time, and during the process killed 7,000 Persians at the loss of 192 Greeks. Xerxes sought to avenge this humiliation that the Greeks cast upon his father and at the same time acquire more territory for his already vast empire. The Persian army numbered over 200,000 and was supported by a naval armada. They set out from Susa, wintered in Sardis where Xerxes sent word demanding the Greeks' surrender and then in the spring of 480 B.C. crossed the Hellespont to begin the invasion proper. Many of the smaller Greek city-states sought peace with Xerxes, but Athens and the Peloponnesian states declined to do so. Recognizing the superiority in numbers of Xerxes' army, the Greeks began devising a strategy to buy time in order to meet the oncoming threat. It was decided to fight a delaying action at Thermopylae because the plain of Thessaly, which served as Xerxes' line of advance, narrowed at this location" on one side were rugged mountains, on the other the ocean. There was no choice for the invading army but to travel through the pass at Thermopylae. Leonidas, one of two Spartan kings, was chosen to defend the pass, and at his command he had a small party of 5,000 men, 300 of which were Spartans, while the other ranks were made up of Peloponnesians, Thebans, and Levies from Phocis and Locris. As Xerxes approached, many of the Greeks began to doubt their ability to defend the pass and held a conference to reconsider their strategy. The Peloponnesians wished to withdraw to the Peloponnese and hold there. The Spartan King Leonidas was appalled at the suggestion and advised staying were they were. As they held their conference a mounted scout from Xerxes' army observed the Greeks who had reconstructed an ancient stone wall that ran across the pass. The Persian horseman could not spy on the 5,000 Greeks, on the wall's far side, but he could see clearly those on his side of the wall. It was the Spartans whom he laid eyes upon, and the site left him very bewildered. They were exercising, talking nonchalantly, and combing their hair. All acted in a most indifferent manner towards their situation. It was almost as if they were on a picnic instead of a battlefield, and in fact they paid the rider no attention even though they were well aware of his presence. Reporting back to Xerxes, the scout told of what he had witnessed, and the Persian king was duly surprised. Summoning Demaratus, an exiled Greek who served as his advisor, Xerxes asked who these men were and what their actions meant. Demaratus said,

When we began out march against Greece, you heard me speak of these men. I told you then how I saw this enterprise would turn out, and you laughed at me. I strive for nothing, my lord, more earnestly than to observe the truth in your presence; so hear me once more. These men have come to fight us for possession of the pass, and for that struggle they are preparing. It is the common practice of the Spartans to pay careful attention to their hair when they are about to risk their lives. But I assure you that if you can defeat these men and the rest of the Spartans who are still at home, there is no other people in the world who will dare to stand firm or lift a hand against you. You have now to deal with the finest kingdom in Greece, and with the bravest men.

— (Knox, *The Norton Book of Classical Literature*, 289)

Xerxes found this answer quite amusing, but in fact it would prove to be an omen of darker days ahead.

Xerxes and his army waited four days, anticipating the Greeks withdrawal. His patience worn thin, the great Persian king finally ordered a frontal assault upon the hoplites. In the front rank of the attack he put the Medes because of their courage, along with the brothers and sons of those who had fallen at Marathon. Xerxes reasoned that their quest for revenge would make this a short lived battle. The force charged across the plain with loud war cries and curses of revenge only to be slaughtered by the Spartans and their allies. Again and again the Medes tried to break though the assembled phalanxes only to fall dead upon the spears and shields of the hoplites. Finally they were pulled from the line by Xerxes and replaced by others who befell the same fate as those before them.

Leonidas' men were all veterans, well-trained and disciplined, their skill was excellent, and Xerxes' dead lay in mute testimony to this. At one point the hoplites hinted at retreat, turning as if to march backwards. The Persians, seeing what appeared to be a withdrawal, came howling at their backs, when at the last moment the Spartans performed an about face, suddenly turning their spears rearward where the enemy impaled themselves upon the weapons' sharp points.[xi] Xerxes, who watched the battle, was furious at its outcome. The area was littered with corpses, most of whom were his own men. It became very clear that although there were many men in his army, none of them were of the quality as those he fought. At the end of the day Xerxes called a halt to the attack, his only accomplishment being the slaughter of his own men. Peter Green observed about the action at Thermoplyae that,

> Yet however determined Xerxes' troops might be, they labored under one insuperable handicap when it came to close-quarters combat: inferiority of weapons and armor. Their spear-javelins, were shorter than those of the Greeks; their large wicker targets, which gave them added mobility over open country, were not protection in a tight-packed, narrow-fronted battle-line. Here the Greeks, with their great body-shields and heavy armor, enjoyed every possible advantage.
> —(Green, *The Greco Persian Wars* 135)

The Persians carried wicker shields, and wore almost no body armor. They relied heavily upon their large bows and preferred to fight from a distance, closing with their opponent only after inflicting losses upon them with their bows, then finishing the engagement with their spear or sword. When forced to fight at close quarters against the Spartans, both their tactics and their equipment proved woefully lacking. Though they did not lack courage, the Persians' skill was no match for the style of fighting to which the Greeks were so accustomed. In their heavy armor, which negated much of the Persians' weaponry, armed with their long spears and deadly *kopis*, the Greeks who fought from the phalanx made short work of Xerxes' men who, although organized into units, fought as individuals and in a disorderly manner.

On the second day of battle much the same happened. Xerxes troops once again died upon the shields and spears of the Greeks who showed no signs of fatigue nor loss of morale. Xerxes grew restless and desperate because his army was backing up on the costal plain, his supplies were growing limited, and his men were worn from both the fighting and the hot summer sun. On that day he learned of a path that led through the mountains and around to the Greeks rear. Recognizing that this was the solution to his woes, the Persian king dispatched a force to traverse the path and attack the Greeks from the rear. Before the battle of Thermopylae, Leonidas, the Spartan king, had dispatched a force of 1,000 Phocians to defend the mountain track. They were surprised by the Persians and withdrew to higher ground to defend themselves. Xerxes' men paid them no more attention and continued onward with their advance to the rear of Leonidas' men.

On the morning of the third day news reached the Greeks that the Persians would soon be at their rear. They once again held a conference to determine the best strategy to deal with this new threat. Many of the Greeks present no longer had a heart to stand and fight, especially considering they were soon to be surrounded. Leonidas deemed it best that those that wanted should retire, however he also decided that the Spartans would defend the pass to buy time for the other Greeks to escape. A few volunteered to stay with the Spartans but the majority withdrew to safety.

As the morning sun rose, Leonidas and his men understood that this would be their last battle. It has been reported that Leonidas ordered his men to eat well that morning for that night they would dine in hell. None of the Spartans had any doubts as to the battle's outcome; all knew their deaths would soon be at hand. Many of them were wounded, their shields were spattered with blood and gore from the past two days of fighting, yet they waited calmly for the Persians to attack once more. Before long, Xerxes' army came. Ahead of them stood the 300 Spartans with their spears and shields at the ready. Leonidas was determined to make the Persians pay heavily for this day, so he ordered his Spartans to attack. Forward they advanced into the open plain, leaving behind the rock wall from which they had fought. As if on parade, the Spartans advanced, spears level, ranks in step, their discipline intact. The sight unnerved many in the lead ranks of Xerxes' force who tried to turn and run, only to be driven back in place by lashes from the Persian commanders' whips. Xerxes' archers began unleashing their deadly barrages and the two armies advanced, colliding once more with blade, spear, and shield. Across the battlefield men cursed, grunted, and screamed as they killed one another at close range; arms and heads were hacked off by swords, intestines spilled to the ground from the twist of a spear, and arrows plummeted downward impaling themselves into any portion of the body not covered by armor.

Leonidas and his men fought that day with reckless abandon for they knew the end was in sight. It was a bloody struggle and soon their spears were broken and their only remaining weapon was the *kopis*. Before long, word came to the Spartans that the Persians had finally come behind them and in an orderly manner they withdrew to the stone wall and there they fought until the last man fell dead from the barrage of arrows unleashed upon him. Xerxes was so angered by the Spartans' resistance that he ordered Leonidas' head be put atop a pole. Demaratus and his observations about the Spartans had proven correct. Not only had the Spartans mauled the Persians physically, but they had also demoralized them. This was only the beginning of what was to be a long and bloody campaign, one that would end in defeat for the Persians a year later at the battle of Plataea where the Spartans would extract revenge for their 300 soldiers who fought and died so bravely at Thermopylae.

In every battle both on land and at sea, the Greeks were outnumbered by the Persians, sometimes by as much as fifty to one. However, the Greeks' martial skills inflicted heavy losses on Xerxes army; even in defeat they were a force to be reckoned with. The Greeks, particularly the Spartans, were a martial culture with a sophisticated means of fighting. From their combative sports, which were practiced in the arena, to the hoplite in his heavy armor on the battlefield, their fighting arts encompassed the entire realm of martial arts. In fact' both their combative sports and battlefield systems were mutually supportive of each other. Although often debated among many Greeks, the hoplite's skills in wrestling, boxing, and *pankration* helped prepare him for the battlefield both physically and mentally. To quote Michael B. Poliakoff who said about the Greeks and their fighting arts,

> Lucian's near contemporary, Philostratos, maintained that the Spartans first developed boxing for military purposes: their warriors did not protect themselves

with helmets, but only a shield, and boxing gave them practice in parrying blows to the head and training in withstanding the ones that did strike home. Reveling in the better days of free Hellas, he adds that the Greeks discovered the military usefulness of pankration and wrestling at the battle of Marathon, when hand-to-hand fighting became necessary, and at Thermopylae, when the beleaguered Spartans snapped their weapons in the fighting and had to continue the battle unarmed.

—(Poliakoff, *Combat Sports*, 96-97)

To develop their fighting skills both on and off the battlefield the Greeks used pre-arranged training routines. They had to, for to defeat an army the size of Xerxes' without a systematic approach to warfare would have been impossible. Hand-to-hand combat was the normal way of fighting in Hellenistic warfare. Therefore, on both individual and at group levels, systematic methods were used to impart combative skills. From a group perspective, the phalanx formation is a pre-arranged training routine that was employed on the battlefield. It was used to not only train the hoplite, but also served as a means to harness the full potential of an armed and armored group of men. It channeled their individual actions, beliefs, and emotions into a highly disciplined and very lethal weapon of war. To quote Victor Davis Hanson, who said about the phalanx, "Like so much of their art and literature, the Greek manner of battle was a paradox of the highest order, a deliberate attempt to harness, to modulate, and hence to amplify if not sanctify the wild human desire for violence through the stark order and discipline of the phalanx." (Hanson, *The Wars of the Ancient Greeks*, 16) The harnessing and amplifying of the wild human desire that Mr. Hanson wrote of is also a motive found within kata practice. The Greeks, who possessed such a skillful martial prowess, were undoubtedly masters of this craft.

1-2 JAPAN AND THE KORYU BUJUTSU

"You should not have a favorite weapon. To become over-familiar with one weapon is as much a fault as not knowing it sufficiently well. You should not copy others, but use weapons that you can handle properly. It is bad for commanders and troopers to have likes and dislikes. These are things you must learn thoroughly." (Musashi, *A Book of Five Rings,* 48)

History has proved to be a double edged sword for the Japanese martial arts or *Koryu bujutsu* as they are traditionally known. For many people today the word 'samurai' invokes images of flashing swords and Japanese warriors dressed in exotic costumes performing acrobatic movements. Perhaps a more esoteric picture comes to mind, one in which the samurai sits engaged in meditation, experiencing some mystical transformation. His sword is not a weapon but instead a vehicle that transports him into a state of enlightenment.

In reality the *Bushi* or warrior class of Japan was many things most of which, it is sad to say, are excluded in our modern day

A PEASANT SOLDIER FIRING THE JAPANESE ARQUABUSE (MATCHLOCK)

visions. The diverse history of the Japanese martial arts could fill volumes, as there were over 700 schools found within them. Although generalizations can be made about the *Koryu bujutsu,* they often prove to be overviews that fail to recognize the uniqueness of each *ryu-ha.* Dr. Karl Friday observed about the *Koryu* that, "Simply put, there is no such thing as a typical or representative martial art *ryu-ha.* To varying degrees, each of the more than 700 schools that scholars have identified is unique in terms of organizational structure and history, strategy, philosophy, and technique. Anyone attempting to formulate general conclusions about traditional Japanese martial art must do so on the basis of some 700 exceptions." (Friday, *Legacies of the Sword,* 9) However, the differences in each *ryu* were not so dramatic as to change the overall conduct of warfare within feudal Japan. Despite the differences in the *ryu-ha's* teachings, being the professional of arms that he was, the samurai was familiar with most, if not all, of the weapons used on the battlefield of his day. If any one generalization is to be made about the samurai, it would be that he is a warrior—a very pragmatic one—who looked upon battle with the eye of a professional soldier.

The samurai fighting arts were designed for the battlefield and composed of several different weapon systems that were often based upon a core set of principles. A samurai was not a specialist in any one system, but instead a warrior proficient in the use of all the tools of his trade; he had to be to survive on the battlefield. Not all of the systems utilized were directly related to combat. Some instead were support systems that helped the warrior in other ways, such as swimming streams in full armor, horsemanship, using signal fires, etc.

The use of the bow and arrow in Japan dates as far back as 750 B.C. Archery was used primarily on foot and on horseback. The samurai's *origins* were that of a horse mounted archer and it was only after he had discharged his arrows that he resorted to the spear or sword, although during the Minamoto *Bakufu* rule, man-to-man dueling on the battlefield was conducted with swords in later periods the warrior's sword was often viewed as a sidearm that was used only when distance or circumstances prevented the employment of pole-arms. This proved especially true in the sixteenth century when the matchlock musket and formations of spearmen dominated the battlefields of Japan. Like the Greek hoplite, the samurai also understood that a lone swordsman stood no chance against a massed group of spearmen who outnumbered him fifty to one, or a line of musket-men whose fire could decimate even the bravest of his countrymen at fifty meters. Author Ellis Amdur wrote about the samurai and his use of the sword, "There is no doubt that brilliant swordsmen using smaller and lighter weapons (*uchigatana*) developed methods of defeating those with heavier and therefore slower weapons. But by-and-large, the sword was a sidearm. Military tactics far superseded brilliance in man-to-man combat with a sword. The preeminent weapons of the Sengoku period battlefield were the spear and projectile." (Amdur, *Keiko Shokon,* 156-157) Despite our modern perceptions of the samurai—many of which have been brought forth by the movie industry—he was not a man to throw away his life needlessly. On the battlefield he waged war with a very calculated eye. He realized that to close with his enemy, he first had to engage them at long range and then "work his way" into sword range. At times this could prove quite impossible, considering the chaotic environment of the feudal battlefield. Therefore, the Japanese man-of-arms was very skilled with other weapons that could kill from a distance, like the bow and arrow and the spear.

With the coming of the Tokugawa period in 1603 the warriors' role was redefined from what it once was. Donn F. Draeger wrote, "Tokugawa's efforts to implement a form of government whose martial arm was wholly defensive led to the fostering of a martial spirit that was both morally hollow and technically unsound. This spirit finally destroyed the society that it was originally intended to serve. The *Bakufu* discouraged martial imagination and inventiveness and in the long run proved hostile to the development and maintenance of martial skill." (Draeger, *Classical Budo,* 16) However, for those samurai of the pre-Tokugawa period, their whole body and mind were trained for combat. Zen and the *bujutsu* became entwined and complimentary to one another. Both stressed learning by experience, words and thoughts could not capture the complete essence of life nor the *bujutsu*. It was only by intuitive means that this could be accomplished. As Christmas Humphreys said about man's thoughts, "The intellect may, and in the West surely must be used, but the user must know the limitations of his chosen tool. The intellect is a magnificent instrument but it has been brightly said that its highest thought will ever be that Truth is beyond all thinking!" (Humphreys, *A Western Approach to Zen,* 140)

JAPANESE SAMURAI

While this process did bring the samurai insights and personal experiences, many of which are unknown to the layman, they were not viewed with the same eye that contemporary practitioners cast toward mysticism. Instead the experience was looked upon as a means that would help the warrior during the chaos and terror of combat. In discussing the relationship of Zen with the samurai, D.T. Suzuki observed that, "Zen discipline is simple, direct, self-reliant, self denying; its ascetic tendency goes well with the fighting spirit. The fighter is to be always single-minded with one object in view: to fight, looking neither backward nor sidewise. To go straight forward in order to crush the enemy is all that is necessary for him. He is therefore not to be encumbered in any possible way, be it physical, emotional, or intellectual." (Suzuki, *Zen and Japanese Culture,* 62) Zen and the Buddhist Marishiten cult both went hand in hand with the predatory nature of the Japanese warrior.[xii] They helped focus and steady his mind for the task at hand, which was battlefield combat. In his examination of human combative behavior, Hoplologist Hunter Armstrong applies a nine point chart developed by D.J. Reis that defines intra- and inter-specific aggressive behavior. The chart is broken down into two categories: Affective and Predatory aggression. Affective behavior traits are more closely related to civilian methods of fighting in which killing your opponent is not always the primary goal. Predatory aggression, by contrast, is directly related to battlefield combat where success is equated with the killing of your enemy. The nine traits identified by Reis in predatory aggression and applied to human combative behavior by Armstrong are:

1. Slight Activation of the autonomous system
2. Stalking
3. Absence of threatening sounds
4. Nape of the prey's neck attacked with teeth
5. No variation in reaction
6. Inter-specific
7. Always directed to success (killing)
8. Related to food intake (or for economical reasons)
9. Very slightly influenced by hormones

Of the nine traits, only two, *Food Intake* and *Inter-Specific,* do not require nor rely upon a state of single-minded concentration. Armstrong wrote about the "No variation in reaction" and its role with the Japanese warrior that: "This too is toward the optimal functioning end of the Imperturbable-mind/Steadfast-mind continuum. While regularly seen in hunting, in inter-personal or group combat, it is a behavioral control that has a genetic set potential that may or may not be attainable via cultural contexts (e.g., upbringing, training). Certainly this condition is recognized as being of primary importance in Japanese combative traditions, and is specifically trained for." (Armstrong, *The Two Faces of Combatives*, 5) When one stops to consider the brutality and intensity of pre-modern warfare in which you often fought your opponent face to face and one mistake could result in a very horrific death, the importance of a steadfast mind can be understood. Although the influences of Buddhism did affect the samurai's character in other ways, aside from those of a combative nature, his primary goal during battle was to kill the enemy; if he reached *satori* during his practice of Zen, so be it, for not only had he reached a state of mind in which he could face death in an unflinching manner, he had also enhanced his combative skills.[xiii]

Although we picture the samurai as brave and honorable warriors who only fought man to man within the code of the *bushido*, they also subscribed to ambushes and assassinations. Dr. Stephen Turnbull describes, "Apart from recounting noble individual deeds of archery duels, challenges, and single combat, the *Gunkimono* also contain many accounts which show how unheroic much of samurai warfare could be. Many battles were carried out by surprise attacks. These involve night raids on buildings, setting them on fire, and indiscriminately slaughtering all who ran out: men, women, and children alike." (Turnbull, *The Samurai*, 29) Like the Europeans who sought and defined a "Just war of the Middle Ages," one which also forbade the killing of non-combatants, the samurai also made exceptions to the rules of conduct governing warfare and they often viewed both the "exception" and its "rule" as one in the same.

The Japanese martial arts evolved from a long history of warfare waged almost entirely within Japan. Unlike the Greeks whose military was composed of common citizens, the Japanese war arts were practiced and perfected by a military aristocracy. The aristocracy grew from commoners but evolved into its own social realm within the Japanese society and would influence the country, its people, and its history for many centuries.

Machiavelli once said, "A prince ought to have no other aim or thought, nor select anything else for his study, than war and its rules and discipline; for this is the sole art that belongs to him who rules, and it is of such force that it not only enables men to rise from a private station to that rank." (Machiavelli, *The Prince*, 66) His statement proves true not only for those warriors of Europe but the samurai as well. The "rules and discipline of war" that Machiavelli spoke of allowed the *Bushi* to rise from a private station to one of rank and rule in Japan. The samurai's sword came to signify many things—loyalty, honor, the duality of life and death—but most of all it symbolized the warrior and all that his life was.

The Birth of Japan and Its Warrior. Like all cultures Japan has its creation myths. One of the earliest accounts of how Japan came to be is recorded in the *Kojiki (Record of Ancient Matters)* and *Nihon Shoki (History of Japan)* both of which were written in the eighth century. According to these accounts, heaven and earth were initially one and the same. There was no separate earth, only a confused molten mass with no form or shape, until a reed shoot sprouted and the mass separated into heaven and earth. Within heaven were two deities, Izanagi and Izanami, who were male and female, respectively. They stood on heaven's floating bridge looking down upon the earth. Taking up a coral spear, they thrust it into the ocean, pulled it out, and then shook it. The drops that fell from its tip formed islands, one of which the couple settled on, building their house, and thus Japan was born.

The land they created was one in which a warrior society could thrive and flourish, and within these earliest records of Japanese history references are made about swordsmanship. Izanagi used a sword to kill his own son, the god of fire, who had inflicted much pain on his mother, Izanami, during childbirth. Aside from ancient mythology, some archaeological digs of imperial mausoleums throughout Japan have made it relatively clear that as far back as the second century B.C. swords were being used in Japan. (Draeger, *Japanese Swordsmanship*, 4)

Weapons systems are not the only means of combat found within the ancient texts of the *Nihon Shoki* and *Kojiki*; unarmed methods of combat are referred to within them as well. Sumo has long been practiced in the Japanese culture and was originally used as a means of ritual warfare whose outcome decided disputes between warring clans. In its ancient form it was a brutal affair that included head butting, striking with both the hands and the feet, and techniques for stomping an opponent to death after they were thrown to the ground. As it was with other premodern cultures, the Japanese recognized the need for fighting skills, arms, and armor.

There are more than 3,000 islands in the Japanese archipelago, which curves 1,200 miles around the northeastern portion of mainland Asia. Rugged mountainous terrain is commonplace in Japan and its islands are close enough to the Asian mainland to allow travel but distant enough to discourage an invasion. These unique geographical features allowed its people to develop a society almost entirely free from outside intervention. The Sea of Japan acted like a castle moat in deterring foreign invaders from Asia. It is believed that the earliest inhabitants of Japan came from the Asian mainland over 10,000 years ago. By 5,000 B.C. pottery making skills had developed. Around 300 B.C. rice farming began and food production methods were slowly being adopted. Within Japan the three largest fertile areas are located on Honshu's eastern shore—the Kanto, Nobi, and Kinai plains. Throughout Japan's history these areas have attracted much of its population and have been the focus of many of its wars.

Along with rice and rice farming techniques, the Japanese adopted both bronze metallurgy and writing from the Chinese (Diamond, *Guns, Germs and Steel,* 333) Japanese culture developed with Chinese influences, but at the same time it developed uniquely Japanese traits. They were not a group of underdeveloped barbarians whose whole society was built upon the Chinese culture. Jared Diamond said about the Chinese influences upon Japan,

> In thus describing China's seminal role in East Asian civilization, we should not exaggerate. It is not the case that all cultural advances in East Asia stemmed from China and that the Koreans, Japanese, and tropical Southeast Asians were noninventive barbarians

who contributed nothing. The ancient Japanese developed some of the oldest pottery in the world and settled as hunter-gatherers in villages subsisting on Japan's rich seafood resources, long before the arrival of food production.

—(Ibid., 333)

In its earliest periods—second to the eighth century A.D.—weapons were both imported and produced in Japan. Many of the swords of this period were straight bladed, much like the ones used on the Asian continent. The swords were both the single edged and double-edged variety. These were very functional weapons and were worn by people of various social levels in Japan. By the seventh century A.D. the foundation upon which the unified Japanese culture was to be built was laid. After being defeated by the Tang armada, Japan pulled its army from Korea and abandoned any hopes of conquering the country (until the seventeenth century). However, the threat of invasion from both China and Korea was growing; in 668 A.D., military training was established for those who lived in Omi province. In 671 A.D., the ranking sovereign Tenji died and a war began over who would succeed him. In reacting to what was believed to be a threat to his rightful position, Tenmu (673-686 A.D) conquered his foes and established his heir to the rule with the use of cavalry and mounted archers. At the same time he began proceedings to establish a conscript army that would be loyal only to him. Tenmu believed that a strong government was established by a strong military, and rightfully so considering the time in history. Thus, martial training was implemented for much of the male populace. Even after his succession, these reforms were continued.

A large part of Tenmu's army was conscripted infantry who were required to serve if between the ages of 20 and 60. They were well trained and equipped, with swords and bows and arrows. One weapon of particular interest used by these conscripts was the *oyumi* or large crossbow, which was issued to each company. It is reputed to have been a very effective weapon that could fire multiple arrows at once. Though the crossbow was more accurate than the bow and arrow, its speed of operation was much slower and by the twelfth century had fallen from use in the Japanese arts of war. The conscripts performed active duty on a rotational basis that in theory was not supposed to keep them away from their lands and families for long periods of time; however, reality was much different and their periods of service proved to be very lengthy and dangerous.

For those who garrisoned in the capital, life could be quite enjoyable, but for those who guarded the frontiers, duty was both harsh and dangerous. In the northeastern frontiers, warfare was a constant affair against the Emishi, a tribal society of Japanese race that resisted any incursions into their lands. The Emishi were very skilled fighters who utilized hit-and-run tactics, ambushes, and raids. They also utilized both the bow and arrow and the sword with great skill, so much so that even imperial Japanese forces suffered many casualties in battles against them. The Emishi were not easily defeated, and to do so took much time and resources from the imperial forces. These frontier wars influenced the evolutionary process of both the samurai and their martial arts. They enabled techniques, tactics and weapons to be developed, all of which would serve as foundations for later martial developments. As Dr. Turnbull said about this period in Japanese history; "These wars, the *Emishi no seibatsu* (the punishment of the Emishi), were particularly important for the development of samurai warfare. In the words of one Japanese historian, they were 'practice for becoming *Bushi*', the term used alternatively for samurai, meaning literally 'military gentlemen'. (Turnbull, *The Samurai,* 13)

In 710 A.D. the first imperial capital was built at Nara. It was during this period that a shift in military thinking began to occur. From the conflicts with the Emishi, who were also skilled in mounted warfare, the role of mounted warriors began to once again reappear in the imperial forces. Likewise, the strain of constant warfare made the need for a professional warrior class apparent. Although the conscripts were equipped and trained they were not able to provide an adequate full-time force. To alleviate the problem, local warlords were commissioned by the emperor to serve as his military force.

In 794 A.D. the capital was moved to Kyoto and this marked

the beginning of the Heian period. The government was largely powerless at this time to protect its people, therefore, it relied upon warriors commissioned to help rule the country. This resulted in the rise of large warrior clans, two of the strongest being the Taira and Minamoto. This appointment of private clans to conduct military affairs ran counter to the Tenmu reforms that sought to control the military under a unified government. The following years were filled with much strife and civil turmoil that was often brought on by power struggles between the large clans.

From these clashes the Taira clan gained control of the government only to be driven from the capital later by the warriors of Minamoto Yoritomo in 1183 A.D. Yoritomo was an intelligent and cautious man. He became the countries first shogun and established a martial government at Kamakura. His was basically a government within a government, one that established the *Bushi,* or warrior, as the undisputed ruler of the land. His government was located at Kamakura; he did not want his warriors to be softened by life in the city of Kyoto as happened with the Taira warriors. Yoritomo stressed martial virtues in his men. Unlike previous rulers he did not prefer one clans' warriors to another; he was only concerned with their loyalty to him, and his only criteria was that they were skilled warriors. He did not use conscripts as others had but instead relied upon those who were professionals at the trade. Donn Draeger wrote,

> Yoritomo avoided conscripting his fighting men, trusting only professional warriors drawn from the ranks of military families or from those select groups most of whose members stemmed from aristocratic blood. He well knew the difference between the conscript and the professional fighting man; whereas the former was a temporary warrior who was forced to submit to martial discipline, the latter was permanently devoted to his profession and willingly subjected himself to its demands. Professional warriors always fought from disciplined habit; they were obedient instruments and thus were dependable under adverse conditions.
>
> —(Draeger, *Classical Bujutsu,* 28)

Yoritomo was well respected by his men, and he ruled them well. He made them lead an uncomplicated existence, be extremely courageous, and train constantly and at times he even determined whom they might or might not marry. His men became the perfect models of the warrior, and they were either loved or hated for their martial prowess. On the battlefield they engaged their foe man to man, each announcing their family lineage, their intention to kill one another, and the method to be used. Once the combat started it only ended with the death of one or both. The seed that had been planted for the warrior class came to bloom under Yoritomo's rule. He appointed his warriors into public offices to police the land, collect taxes, and enforce laws. In effect, he built the foundation upon which the warrior class would stand to rule Japan—one he would not live to see. In 1199 A.D. Yoritomo was thrown from his horse and died shortly thereafter from injuries he sustained. He was succeeded by the Hojo family who initially sustained a stable government but whose control in time began to fade because they could not win the respect of the warrior class as Yoritomo had. The warriors became distanced from the *Bakufu* due to its policies and their inability to influence events as they once had during Yoritomo's rule. The *Bushi's* loyalty began to erode and the Shogun's control over them began to slip. The country was slowly edging towards feudal warfare postponed only briefly by an army of invaders who came from across the sea.

The Mongols and the Rise of *Bujutsu*. In 1238 A.D. the English chronicler Matthew Paris wrote of a menace that was threatening Europe, a race of people who were inhuman, in their actions and of monstrous appearance,

> The men are of the nature of beasts. They thirst after and drink blood. They clothe themselves in the skins of bulls and are armed with iron lances. They are short in stature and thick-set, compact in their bodies. Their horses are very swift and able to perform a journey of three days in one. They have swords and daggers and one edge-sabers-and are excellent archers.

> They take their herds with them, as also their wives,
> who are brought up to war the same as the men. Their
> chief is a ferocious man named Khan.
> —(Newark, *Warlords*, 134-135)

They came from the steppes of central Asia, a hearty warlike people who outrode and outfought almost everyone who stood in their way. In 1207 A.D. the Mongols took control of southern Siberia, in 1223 A.D. they defeated a Kievan army and pillaged Transcaucasia, and in 1236 A.D. they crossed the Urals and set Moscow ablaze. In April of 1241 A.D. the Poles were defeated and the victorious Mongols cut off the right ear of every dead Polish prince on the battlefield. Afterwards they stormed into Hungry and performed similar acts of terror. Such a large area had never before been controlled by one military force. The Mongols committed atrocities in the blink of an eye, murdered innocent people at a whim, and yet at the same time practiced a sophisticated method of warfare through which they conquered much of Asia and Europe. On two separate occasions they tried to conquer Japan and both times were defeated.

In 1259 A.D. Kublai Khan, grandson of Genghis Khan, became Emperor of China and five years later he relocated his capital to the city of Beijing. At this time the borders of his empire were well within sailing distance to Japan, so in 1268 A.D. he sent envoys to Japan with a letter that basically stated, "either open trade with us or you will be invaded." The Japanese were both infuriated and startled by the letter. The Mongol envoys left without the desired reply and Japan promptly began preparing for war. Khan attempted, over the course of the next few years, to open diplomatic talks with the Japanese, but in every case his efforts were rebuked. In November of 1274 A.D. the Mongol fleet set sail for Japan and landed at Imazu on the 19th day of that month. The next day the Mongols attacked Hakata and a royal battle ensued between them and the samurai.

The style of fighting employed by the Mongols was different from that of the Japanese. For the samurai, engaging in single combat with a foe on the battlefield was the most desired and accepted method. Although the idea of this ritualistic combat may have been stronger than the stark reality of combat, it was a tradition still sought by the samurai. The tradition consisted of stating your family's lineage, as well as your own murderous intentions, before engaging in combat. However, for the Mongols no such lofty ideas existed; they were masters of the art of massed formations. They had not won their conquests in Asia and Europe by individual combats but instead by mass volleys of arrows and large formations of spearmen who saw no dishonor whatsoever in killing a lone warrior by overwhelming odds. It was the courage and individual skills of the samurai that won the day against the Mongols and the one weapon, that shone brightest was the samurai's sword. Engaging their enemy at close quarters, the Japanese warriors inflicted a terrible price upon the invaders who were surprised by the resistance they encountered. The Japanese were forced to retreat behind fortifications built some 600 years earlier and await reinforcements. The Mongols had not come expecting a prolonged engagement; the fighting had depleted their supplies and they withdrew to their ships, setting fire to the villages that stood at the water's edge. A typhoon struck the Mongol fleet as it was departing the bay, destroying many ships and killing nearly 13,000 of the invaders. Seven years later the Mongols would once again return, this time with a larger army. And once again they would be defeated by the samurai's skill at arms and by the help of another typhoon—"the divine wind," or Kamikaze as the Japanese called it. Following the Mongol invasions, war was to become common place for almost three centuries as Japan entered the chaotic Ashikaga period of 1336-1568 A.D. It was an era ripe with warfare, and during this time great strides in the development of martial arts systems was seen. The power of both the Shogun and the *Bakufu* left the country without any central control, as a result power was in the hands of local warlords. From this vacuum rose both the *daimyo* and the martial *ryu*.

The *daimyo* were large landowners who had risen to power and ruled their holdings and those who lived on their lands with absolute control. The memory of the Mongols was not left at the water's edge by the *daimyo*. It was not long before the employment of foot soldiers in massed formations came into use in Japan. To protect their domains, the *daimyo* began to recruit farmers and peasants into their own private armies. They became known as *Nobushi* or *Ji-Samurai*. Although they were given instruction in the use of arms, extensive training such as the samurai received was not required mainly because of their social standing and the massed formations used. They were, however, worthy fighters who would play a great role in future events. With the increased use of infantry, different types of terrain that prohibited use of horses, and massed formations that also made cavalry charges impractical, the samurai began to fight on foot, and in doing so his sword reflected, the changes on both the battlefield and in his social standing. He began to carry two swords to distinguish him from the commoner who carried only one; his long sword, the *tachi*, was replaced by a shorter, and more agile blade called the *katana*. This resulted in a more refined method of swordsmanship and the samurai's study of the sword's use took on new meaning to him. As Mr. Draeger wrote about this period, "Realistic warriors fighting on foot came to the awakening that a lighter and shorter curved blade could almost be manipulated with greater speed and, if properly used, was capable of almost the same lethal penetration as that of heavier swords when used against armor. The significance of this discovery is that the acceptance of a lighter-weight sword stimulated a more systematic study of swordsmanship along lines of finesse in technique." (Draeger, *Japanese Swordsmanship*, 13)

Formalized methods of training had existed in Japan for many years. Like the Greeks, the Japanese also recognized that the better trained the warrior, the more likely his chances of survival, therefore standardized methods of training evolved. It was during the thirteenth century that these techniques were organized into very systematic and structured methods called *ryu-ha*. Although the teachings of the *ryu-ha* were centered on the weapons most commonly used—bow, spear, and sword—they did not exclude other methods of combat such as grappling, use of the dagger, and striking with empty hands or *atemi*, which although studied was not a primary means of fighting since the samurai's combat was conducted with weapons and in armor. The *ryu* was literally an immersion into the realms of combat, That trained the warrior on both a physical and mental plane. Each *ryu* had its own identity, teachings and techniques, that differed from others. The purpose of all classical *ryu-ha* was the training and preparation of the warrior for combat. These were not methods that sought to preserve techniques for the sake of preservation alone. Instead, the techniques and teachings were preserved because they had proven themselves effective in mortal combat. The tradition of the *ryu* was based on the warrior's current needs. As it is with the modern day infantryman who does not alter the shape of his rifle, so it was with the samurai who did not alter the *ryu's* teachings. They were preformed in a prescribed manner because of their functionality and not their aesthetic appeal; the *ryu-ha* existed to pass this knowledge to the warrior who, through diligent practice, would develop physical skill.[xiv] To quote Dr. Karl Friday who said about the *ryu-ha* and their teachings, "They exist not to foster physical skills but to hand on knowledge. For skill cannot be taught or learned—it can only be acquired through long training and practice." (Friday, *Legacies of the Sword,* 58)

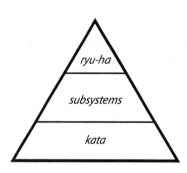

THE ILLUSTRATION IS AN EXAMPLE OF THE RYU'S ORGANIZATION. YOU HAVE THE RYU ITSELF, COMPOSED OF VARIOUS SUB-SYSTEMS—SWORD, NAGANATA, SPEAR, ETC.— AND THEN THE KATA, OR FOUNDATION.

The *ryu-ha* were designed as a pyramid. There was the *ryu* itself, and then the sub sections of it, which were the various systems it was comprised of, such as *kenjutsu* (sword-skills), *sojutsu* (spear-skills), *kyujutsu* (bow and arrow) techniques, and others that pertained to combat.

The base of the *ryu's* teachings rests upon kata or prearranged exercises. These allowed the samurai to practice the *ryu's* techniques in a repetitive manner, which then could be applied to any given situation the warrior found himself in. The *ryu's* kata were done in two-person sets and realistically depicted the engagement of armed men, however it allowed the practitioners to do so safely. Free sparring, which is so popular among modern fighting arts practitioners, could not and would not be practiced due to the nature of the *Koryu bujutsu*. These systems relied heavily upon weapons and their practice was conducted with live blades between two people, with one acting as the attacker and the other as the defender. A mistake on either side could prove fatal. Likewise, the flamboyant movements often seen in modern forms of free sparring are very much opposed to those movement patterns practiced in the *Koryu bujutsu*. These are systems designed to be used on broken terrain and in harsh conditions where good solid footing was essential for survival. The samurai also fought in armor; therefore, the kata's techniques were designed to be simple but effective.

By practicing the katas techniques constantly, the samurai developed behavioral patterns that allowed him to execute the techniques under the stress of combat. It was this extremely efficient means of organizing and practicing the *bujutsu*, along with the warrior ethos, that made the samurai one of the most respected men-of-arms known to mankind. However, the method used by the Japanese to define, organize, practice, and transmit their martial arts is not exclusive to their culture.

The process of codification, systematization and transmission of a martial art can be found within many cultures. One of the greatest reasons for these methods of systematization was the transmission of martial knowledge from one warrior to another. Having knowledge of techniques was often as important as physical skill and the means to preserve and transmit this knowledge was accomplished not only by kata but also through poetry, writing, folktales, and dancing.

There are three basic methods of transmitting information from one person to another. They are: to make use of sound, such as talking, singing, reciting folktales and poetry; to make use of illustrations, which would include words, drawing and pictures; and through physically based movements such as dancing and kata. Prior to our modern age, information was transmitted only as fast as a man traveled. Therefore all three of these methods were used to not only send information but to assimilate and store it. Though considered somewhat primitive by our modern standards of communication, they were effective and in some cases more so than our current methods.

CHAPTER 2

Inspiration and Transmission of the Warrior's Way

The method of back-sword play was handed down by a succession of professors, who learned it partly by rote, but mostly by practical experience (for of books there were very few indeed), and down to the end of the eighteenth century there were practically no changes in it.

—Alfred Hutton

Knowledge is power; this has never been as true as it is within the ranks of the warrior. The means to communicate and transmit knowledge has often been a deciding factor in the course of history. When the Spaniards came to the New World, written accounts of Columbus's expeditions and Cortez's conquering of Mexico spurred others to follow in their paths. Likewise, the ability to communicate through written word helped the Spaniards greatly in defeating the Inca Empire. The Incas had no literary tradition in their society as did the Spaniards; they knew nothing about the Spaniards or their intentions. Unlike the Spaniards, who did have such traditions, which gave them great insight into not only history, but also a long example of combative behavior and tactics that had been proven through the course of many wars. They used this with great effect to defeat the Incas. At the battle of Cajamarca, Peru in 1532, a force of Spaniards numbering less than 200 men defeated an Inca army numbering close to 80,000 without the loss of one Conquistador. (Diamond, *Guns, Germs and Steel,* 75-80)

2-1 POETRY, ZEN, AND THE WARRIOR'S ETHOS

Aside from the transmission of knowledge pertaining to techniques and tactics, literary traditions have aided the warrior in preparing themselves mentally for battle by helping induce mental states through rhythmic chants and symbolic meanings that were attached to certain letters, phrases, and passages. While discussing the use of *mudras* and *mantras*[xv] in 'Japanese Bujutsu', David A. Hall stated that,

> Hand-to-hand combat anywhere in the world requires a strong will. If a participant in a battle had performed a ritual that makes him psychologically stronger (i.e., more confident in himself and his fighting ability), he will be a more formidable opponent to face. One example of this is the use of the kuji (nine mystic letters) and the juji (ten mystic letters) by such traditions as the Katori Shinto Ryu. By inscribing the proper ideographic character upon one's hands, weapons and so on, protection of various types may be obtained.
>
> —(Hall, *Hoplos,* Nov. 1979 Vol. 1, No. 6)

This tradition, however, was not only found within Asian cultures but also European martial traditions. Many old English poems have their roots in the German heroic traditions where legends that were handed down orally were also used in a martial context. Often the poems would tell of an ancient hero's exploits on the battlefield and would serve as an example of the warrior's courage and martial prowess.

Thor was one of the early Germanic hero-gods and it was common for Germanic warriors to march off to battle singing war songs about him. Just prior to the start of battle, they would begin chanting a war cry or *barritus*. The purpose of both the song and war cry was twofold; they helped instill and maintain the warrior tradition, and the various tones used within the *barritus* helped prepare the warrior mentally for battle. The *barritus* was almost hypnotic in its chanting, and some even believed that through it the outcome of the battle could be foreseen. Author C.L. Wrenn wrote about the use of the German war cry, "This *barritus* inflames the minds of the warriors to war; and by its varying tones the fortunes of the impending battle may be discovered by divination. In this recitation, "harshness of sound and a kind of rhythmic rising and falling are especially aimed at, as the sound of the voices is made to swell out more fully and with more powerful weight through the repercussion caused by placing men's shields in front of their faces." (Wren, *Study of Old English Literature,* 75) Often the division between martial and literary traditions was non-existent in the pre-modern warrior's day. Though his skill with sword and spear were good, he never failed to fortify himself mentally through the use of songs, chants, stories and poems.

Prior to the industrial age, poetry was a metaphor of life for the English. It captured the unseen, unspoken essence of the universe and then placed it in front of man for him to examine. Poetry was the kata of words and it allowed man to understand the world and those who lived in it, not in fragmented ideas, but instead in a continuous process where all events intersected and influenced one another. However, with the dawn of the industrial age, a mechanistic philosophy that was born during the Enlightenment began to influence man's world. Its rigid framework reduced a history of rationalism that had been the foundation for the arts, music, literature, and even the fighting arts to one of a fragmented and mechanically dependent experience that was very static and often un-evolving in terms of the human perspective.[xvi] As William H. Marshall said about the era and the Industrial Age's effects on not only poetry but mans world views, "The mimetic function that earlier poetry had served now ceased to be really meaningful to many literary figures, for in any given case if the poet felt that he no longer understood the nature and structure of the universe, he could hardly write a poem imitating and explaining these.

At the beginning of the nineteenth century, therefore, each thinking, creative mind was in large measure left in isolation." (Marshall, *The Major English Romantic Poets,* xxvii) As English society changed from an agrarian way to that of an industrial one so to did its rituals, traditions, and values. This was true for not just the English, but for many other societies, and as time passed the influences of the industrial age came to have greater impact on man and the world he lived in. Often, time-honored traditions like those of the craftsman, artist and poet—once held in high esteem by society—came to be replaced by modern ideas that valued quantity instead of the variety of life.

In our world today, with its contemporary segmentation process that compartmentalizes each and everything into independent entities that have no relation to one another, we often view the roles of the warrior, poet, writer, and artist as separate endeavors, that never cross paths. However, in earlier societies, they were at times one and the same. Man's earliest ambitions was to describe the word in which he lived, and that world was often filled with wars. Thus his verse and prose often reflected upon war, its frustrations, and the frailty of life, which he faced so often on the field of battle. The eighth century Chinese poet Chen Shen recorded his own experiences of battle in 756 A.D. when he wrote, "Following the Army on Campaign". In the poem he describes the horror of war and his own feelings towards it:

> I venture to sorrow for my life.
> At forty I am not yet old.
> One morning civil war began;
> Each day our lives uncertain.
> The Tartar troops have taken Chang'an;
> Within palace chambers wild weeds grow.
> I'm heartbroken for the trees of Wuling:
> I no longer see the capital's boulevards.
> My Sovereign is with marching troops;
> Arms and horses are everywhere.
> The Tartar rebels are not yet quelled:
> Earnestly the many commanders subjugate them.
> Recently I heard of Xianyang's fall;

In the massacre all swept clean.
A mass of corpses piled like a hillock:
Oozing blood swells this land of Feng and Hao.
Shields and spears impede my homeland;
Jackals and tigers all over the citadel's walls.
Villages and hamlets without any man.
Desolate the mulberry and date trees.
The scholar has a far reaching plan,
But there is no place to express his innermost
thoughts.
Alone, there is a man lamenting for his time;
Lifting his head he wails to the blue sky.
—(Chan, *Chen Shen*, 10)

Although much blood was spilt as Chen Shen's poem shows, he still lamented about his own lack of expertise in the arts of war; partially because his deficiencies did not gain him recognition and partially because he felt insignificant and unable to extract revenge from his enemies. This does not mean that he was unfamiliar with the arts of war, merely that he was not as skilled as those who had practiced them from childhood.

The warrior often played dual roles, one being the protector of his society, the other being the memory of it. Stephen Pollington observed about the Germanic warrior that, "Germanic warriors were not brutish louts; they respected skill with words as much as skill at arms, and they valued the good reputation and lasting memory the poet could confer." (Pollington, *The English Warrior,* 67) When a man's emotions are stirred he seeks to express them in some manner, and of all his experiences war and love are the most intense; love is the giver of life and the other, war, the taker of life. Within war and all its horror, man found death, glory, honor, courage, and at times, the meaning to life itself. In his literary traditions he sought to record and express these feelings along with the more technical aspects of his craft, such as the use of swords, spears, and cavalry. Through poetry, song and verse he even addressed the proper mindset that the warrior should have when entering battle, and he passed this knowledge to others. The great swordsman Miyamoto Musashi once wrote, "In strategy your

MEDIEVAL KNIGHT

spiritual bearing must not be any different from normal. Both in fighting and in everyday life you should be determined though calm. Meet the situation without tenseness yet not recklessly, your spirit settled yet unbiased. Even when your spirit is calm do not let your body relax, and when your body is relaxed do not let your spirit slacken." (Musashi, *Book of Five Rings,* 53) Chaucer, Machavelli, Sir Philip Sidney, Chen Shen and others also wrote about the warrior his mindset and skill of arms. Perhaps some of the most dramatic accounts of early warfare and testaments to the warrior's steadfast state of mind can be found in *The Alliterative Morte Arthur* and its account of Sir Gawain's battle against Sir Modred and his knights, Gawain charges a foe that outnumbers him considerably with a heart full of vengeance and his hand clasped firmly around his sword. Charging atop his steed the brave knight is both lethal and inspiring; he is the perfect role model of the warrior in the thick of combat:

> There no man stop him, his reason was gone.
> He fell in a frenzy through fierceness of heart;
> He fights and fells down him who stands before him.
> There befell never a doomed man such a fortune on earth.
> In the whole battle headlong he runs him,
> And hurts the hardiest of men that move upon the earth;
> Raging like a lion he lunges throughout them,
> These lords and leaders who wait on the land.
> Still Sir Gawain in his woe wavers but little,
> But wounds his opponents with wonderful dints,
> As one who willfully would waste himself;
> And through his pain and his will all his wits failed him,
> That mad as a wild beast he charged at the nearest;
> All wallowed in blood where he had passed by;
> Each man could be wary at the vengeance of others.
> —(Morte, *Medieval Verse,* 145)

The passage "As one who willfully would waste himself" is a reflection on the steadfast mind that was so essential to the pre-modern warrior and his performance on the field of battle. In describing the differences between English and Japanese poetry and their respective trains of thought Robert Hass wrote, "When Wordsworth or Keats writes about being 'in pensive or in wayward mood', you know that they're doing one of the jobs of the artist, trying to assimilate psychological states for which the official culture didn't have a language. Basho's Japan did." (Hass, *The Essential Haiku*, xiv) This is one of the undercurrents within the Arthurian poem and many others of the European traditions. Although they did not have an official term to describe Zen, the steadfast state of mind was still present, still used, and referred to often within the traditions of European literature. By not having an official term it is quite possible that the Europeans captured the essence of the "steadfast mind state" as completely, if not more so, than those practicing formal methods of Zen. For words do not always capture the true essence of a subject as Kenneth Yasuda pointed out when he wrote, "If Fletcher's thought is carried further, it can be shown that the Imagists, with their concern for 'what could be pictorially and vividly stated,' had forgotten that the naming of objects alone does not constitute an image." (Yasuda, *The Japanese Haiku*, xviii) This is not just Yasuda's viewpoint. The early Jewish mystics felt that God's presence could not be comprehended nor captured in the utterance of a few simple words. God instead was a force that could be alluded to, but whose majesty was meant to be experienced and not discussed in simplistic terms. The European man-of-arms did understand and experience the steadfast mind state, just as did his Japanese and Chinese counterpart. His fighting arts employed no official term for it outside of those found within his religious doctrines or cultures expressions. Wrote Richard Hayes about the experience of steadfastness and its relation to all men-of-arms that: "In the combative context or milieu, whether Roman legion in Gaul, Japanese *Bushi* in the Kamakura era, the Blue and the Grey in the American Civil War, or amid more recent instances of human conflict, the imperturbable-mind/steadfast-mind trait allows us to perform with a clear sensorium in the very face of death." (Hayes, Hoplos, Fall 1988) With a martial history as long and distinguished as that of Western societies, it is a natural conclusion to draw that its men-of-arms were well aware of what is commonly referred to today as the "Zen state".

In many ways the literary traditions are kata-like because they have set examples for the man-of-arms on how he should both fight and conduct himself during his daily affairs. Grappling skills and weapons play have long gone hand in hand with one another, as Castiglione showed when he wrote of the two and their use together in the first *Book of the Courtier*, "I thinke also it will serve his turne greatly, to know the feat of wrastling, because it goeth much together with all weapon on foote." (Castiglione, *Book of the Courtier*, 40) By "wrastling" Castiglione did not mean our contemporary versions of Olympic style Greco-Roman or WWE but instead an intricate and sophisticated means of dealing with an opponent, one not unlike those systems of *jujutsu* used in feudal Japan that were designed to subdue an enemy long enough to dispatch him with your sword or knife. Castiglone also wrote about when and when not to make use of martial prowess and that a constant state of warfare was not proper or ethical for man. He stated that, "Even as therefore in war they ought to bend their people to the profitable and necessarie vertues to come by the end (which is, peace) so in peace, to come by the end (which is quitnesse) they ought to bend them to honest vertues, which be the end of the profitable." (Ibid., 281)

Aside from Castiglione and the European martial arts, poetry, song and verse also were used extensively in Asian martial arts. It was not uncommon for early Chinese martial arts practitioners to be unable to read or write, therefore much information was passed on through poetry and folktales, just as in early European cultures. For the Chinese, poems and songs contained the essence of their fighting art and were only passed on to the most worthy and reliable practitioners. Dr. Yang, Jwing- Ming stated about these forms of verse and the role played by them in the Chinese fighting arts that, "These songs and poems, which contain the theory, training methods, key points, and above all the experiences accumulated over the past few centuries, provide *Baguazhang* practitioners with excellent guidelines for their training. They are the essence and root of the Baguazhang style. If your practice diverges from these guidelines, then it should not be classified as Baguazhang." (Yang, Liang, Wu, *Baguazhang,* 53) Although primarily warriors, many were also poets and scholars; through them the tradition of the pen and sword was born. As Musashi once wrote, "It is said the warrior's is the twofold Way of pen and sword, and he should have a taste for both Ways." (Musashi, *Book of Rings,* 37)

2-2 POETRY, WRITTEN WORDS, AND THE SCHOLAR WARRIOR

From man's earliest beginnings, the use of sound as communication has been of great importance. In pre-historic times before any formal language was established, sounds were used to communicate. What exactly brought forth the development of language remains somewhat of a mystery even to this day. However, it is speculated that somewhere between 50,000 and 100,000 years ago our human bodies evolved so that we could make coherent sounds in a repetitive manner. Thus the foundations of language were established—as well as the means by which we communicate, establish our customs and beliefs, and exercise our creativity. (Diamond, *Guns, Germs and Steel,* 40) Many of the first spoken words were of a one syllable variety and were used in conjunction with the surroundings where a particular group of humans lived. This is not to say that geography was the sole deciding factor in linguistic evolution. Early man's concerns were those most immediate to him; therefore, words evolved to suit his needs. If a predator such as a lion, tiger, or wolf was one of his immediate concerns, then a word to describe the predator came to be. Likewise, words were developed for food and water, which were also immediate concerns.

Soon early man realized he could combine his simple words into more complex ones, that would have greater meaning. He also came to the conclusion that he could arrange his words together and greater amounts of information could be transmitted. In doing so he also noticed through the linking of several words that a rhythm of sound was emitted that consisted of various tones. Before long, established patterns of speech evolved that were based on tonal variations and changes in pitch, volume, and accent. In time, as his vocabulary grew, he used it to describe emotions, events, etc. From the rhythmical patterns of his language, folktales, songs, and poetry were developed, it was satisfying for man to hear these sounds that described events, people and places being recited in a rhythmical manner. They could be soothing at times while on other occasions they could be inspiring, enraging, and even used to drive men into a warlike state of mind.

Poetry evolved along with language because of the rhythmic nature of speech, which man found not only satisfying but also in accord with the world in which he lived. It ebbed and flowed as the seasons and was often fused with music. It was a primitive rhythm that he found pleasurable, one that came from his very soul. Thus the experience of language soon became one of an aesthetic nature. It helped man explore realms that were within him, and became a tool in which he could describe, categorize, and even analyze his own feelings. C.L. Wrenn stated about poetry that, "It follows, therefore, that it is in their poems that men develop most fully and naturally the inner and individual qualities of their language, and that aesthetic excellences, if found at all, are to be sought in the verse rather than the prose of an early stage of literature." (Wrenn, *Study of English Literature,* 35) In time it became the poet who would record the history of a people for it was the sequence and rhythm of his verse that allowed him to recall and recite the information he had stored in his memory. For many cultures, poetry is the earliest recorded history known. Nora Chadwick said of Ireland and her traditions that, "Although late in acquiring the art of writing, and indeed partly because of this, she had developed an advanced body of oral tradition in which were preserved traditions dating from several centuries prior to their committal to writing." (Chadwick, *The Celts,* 255) And indeed this proved true for not only the Celts but others as well where verse was the first means of recording history.

Early poetry reflected not only the events themselves but also conveyed the feelings of those who were involved and gave in many ways a much more in-depth view of those events than what is found in modern history books. In the epic poem *Beowulf,* the hero of the story is toasted at a night's festival that is all gaiety until the realization that, that very night, their enemy—the dreaded Grendel—will come stalking those who are present at the festivities:

> Then it was like old times in the echoing hall,
> proud talk and the people happy,
> loud and excited; until soon enough
> Halfdane's heir had to be away
> to his night's nest. He realized
> that the demon was going to descend on the hall,
> that he plotted all day, from dawn-light
> until darkness gathered again over the world
> and stealthy night-shapes came stealing forth
> under the cold murk.
> —(Heaney, *Beowulf, A New Translation*, 642-650)

Not only does this passage explain the mood of the people but also it also describes their actions, the weather, and that the demonic Grendel had plotted all day, even until that very night to kill them. In addition one can also sense the mood swing of the people through the rhythm and tone of the poem. Although this is in written form, one can only imagine its effect if recited in old English and accompanied by the music of 1,000 years ago. Each verse conjured up images and feelings to those who heard them. There was a depth to the verse, one in which each word had a layered meaning that encompassed not only information, but also emotions, sounds, scents, geographical locations and even the attitudes held by various groups of people. In the Icelandic tale *Egil's Saga* when the word *berserks* is used, it denotes a particular type of Norse warrior who, although held in high regard for their fighting prowess, were feared by many due to their state of mind and actions during combat. Ewart Oakeshott wrote of them, "This seems to have been usual *Berserk* practice before a fight, to work themselves up into that sort of psychopathic frenzy which makes men quite impervious to caution or pain or any thought at all save the will to slay. Very terrifying it must have been, and effective." (Oakeshott, *The Archaeology of Weapons*, 157)

There was also power in language. Many early haiku masters believed that words were units of energy that when spoken could have effect on time, space and people. The Irish believed that words could alter the physical world through the energy of their vibrations; a man who cursed another could bring bodily harm through the power of his words. Therefore to condemn or damn another person was not a task taken lightly. The experience of verse was one that impacted people deeply. Verse encompassed not only communicative elements but also cultural, geographical, and spiritual ones and was embedded with both a power and meaning that went far beyond the mere utterance of words.

For those who lived in the Pre-Modern martial arts era, poetry captured the human experience completely; it was a medium that allowed people to explore and understand the world in which they lived both mentally and spiritually. Skill in verse was not an endeavor that was looked upon lightly by those who possessed it. The legendary Japanese poet Basho observed about the old masters of Haiku, that so demanding was the art form they would compose only one or two great poems in their lifetimes. Kenneth Yasuda wrote of Haiku, and the fact that an object's name alone does not carry forth its image that, "As the Japanese poets have tried to remember, the totality of the poem is the image, within which there may be one or more objects." (Yasuda, *The Japanese Haiku*, xviii) Poetry, therefore reflected not only the history of a culture's people, but the feelings and emotions that were bound with that history. Though at times it is abstract and metaphorical in its presentation, poetry nonetheless was and still is a literal living, breathing, means of transmission that conveys its events in a multi-dimensional way in which the individuals are forced to participate if they are to reap its benefits and understand its message.

The advent of the written word came long after man's ability to make use of speech. Civilizations had to first mature and then advance in their intellectual capabilities before written forms of communication were developed. C.L. Wrenn stated about the development of prose after verse that, "It is, so to speak, a law of nature that the oral making of verse arises early in the history of a people's culture, whereas prose can only develop in a relatively maturing state of civilization when the art of writing, as distinct from oral tradition, has begun to serve utilitarian and didactic purposes." (Wrenn, *Study of Old English Literature,* 35) The development of the written word was a complex and difficult endeavor, for not only did man have to develop signs that represented various words and their meanings, but he also had to take into account the various tonal differences found within the spoken language and incorporated them into his newly formed prose. Jared Diamond wrote of the task and its enormity that, "Somehow, the first scribes solved all those problems, without having in front of them any example of the final result to guide their efforts. That task was evidently so difficult that there have been only a few occasions in history when people invented writing entirely on their own." (Diamond, *Guns, Germs, and Steel,* 218)

Cuneiform is one of the earliest forms of writing known and was developed by the Sumerians in the fourth and fifth centuries B.C. It initially consisted of logograms that represented various objects such as cows, sheep, slaves, and other items of importance to the ruling class of the day. Early forms of writing, like cuneiform, were not used for aesthetic purposes, but instead for accounting. Writing was a skill limited to the ruling class people who realized its significance and established records and accounts that could wield them more control. This was also true with the Egyptian hieroglyphic script, proto-India Script, both Cretan and Chinese script, as well as others. It was only later in history when written vocabulary began to expand that it spread to those outside of the ruling class and was used for other purposes other than an official nature. In time the written word came to be used to record folklore, legends, poetry and other traditions that had previously only been stored and transmitted orally. The same symbolism, myths, and metaphors that were used in verse were also employed in prose, as many felt that mere words alone could not capture the true nature of a subject.

Literature can exist without writing; however, a language that has no written form of preserving and transmitting its linguistic artifacts runs the risk of loosing these traditions if they are not recorded. The culture itself runs the risk of being forgotten if some record of its existence not be maintained. Much of our knowledge of the ancient Celts was gained through Roman and Greek accounts, and much of it relates to their martial prowess, which both the Greeks and Romans experienced first hand. However it was not because of a language barrier between the three cultures that the accounts of early Celtic civilization may seem vague, but instead because the ancient Celts had no written means to store or transmit knowledge about their society, and much of their culture's heritage has gone undiscovered.[xvii] To quote Nora Chadwick, "The linguistic barrier was insignificant; but because of the lack of written communication the accumulated knowledge of the ancient world was a closed book to Celtic peoples, and the history, the intellectual life, the mythology and religious experience, the eloquence and art of the formal speech of the Celts were little known to the Greeks and Romans." (Chadwick, *The Celts*, 43) Thus with the development of writing, man had a method of both storing and transmitting information in an original unaltered form. He could recall past events in a detailed account, he could also record current events and commit to prose those ideas and feelings that stirred him. He could now record those techniques and tactics that had served him so well on the battlefield.

Probably some of the oldest examples of preserving and transmitting information pertaining to the fighting arts can be found with the ancient Egyptians, who with their hieroglyphics recorded scenes of wrestlers utilizing various techniques. By the turn of the fifteenth century manuscripts that dealt with not only the techniques used but also the philosophies of both war and weapons were becoming commonplace in both Asian and European societies. Sun Tzu's, *The Art of War*, was believed to have been written around 480-221 B.C., the same time in history that Socrates, Plato, and Aristotle were laying the foundation of what was to become Western Philosophy. The philosophical traditions of the Asian world would influence in the study of their martial arts. During Japan's Tokugawa period, philosophical traditions, cultural mores, and the warrior ethos would combine into the code of the *bushido*. It was a work that was to become a medium through which martial prowess and civil laws could work together without conflict, although in later years its misinterpretation would lead many astray from its true intent and purpose.

In Western traditions it was St. Augustine who, inspired by the Old Testament, would combine Roman and Judaeo-Christian elements into the Just War doctrine. This was a treatise that influenced warfare and those who studied it throughout the history of Europe. As Frederick H. Russell wrote about Augustine's view towards war and the use of arms, "Central to his attitude was the conviction that war was both a consequence of sin and a remedy for it. The real evils in war were not war itself but the love of violence and cruelty, greed and the *libido dominandi* or lust for rule that so often accompanied it." (Russell, *The Just War,* 16) Although St. Augustine's treatise was not accepted by every man-of-arms due to its complicated nature, his thoughts and ideas nevertheless influenced the European martial arts and their accompanying manuscripts. Hans Talhoffer's fifteenth century sword-fighting manual, Castiglione's *The Book of the Courtier*, Machiavelli's *The Prince*, and other works that explored both the technical and philosophical sides of combat have all been influenced by the Just War precept.[xviii] Both Castiglione and Machiavelli explored the martial arts from a courtly view that encompassed ethics, martial philosophy, strategy, conduct and the role of the warrior in society.

Castigilone's *The Book of the Courtier* was first published in 1528 A.D. and expressed the fact that the scholar and warrior were one and the same. It is a work considered to be a masterpiece of Italian Renaissance literature, and within it the author gives much insight into how the courtier's training should be conducted from both a physical and mental perspective. Castigilone, a man of his day and age, was skilled in the use of arms. In writing his book, Castiglione provided much insight into not only Renaissance life but also the role played by the martial arts during that period of time. One passage in particular shows that the Courtier should be prepared to use his martial skills both on and off the field of battle. As Castigilone stated,

"For beside the use that he shall have of them in warre, where peradventure needeth no great cunning, there happen oftentimes variances betweene one gentleman and an other, whereupon ensueth a combat. And many times it shall stand him in steade to use the weapon that he hath at that instant by his side, therefore it is a very sure thing to be skilfull." (Castiglione, *The Book of the Courtier*, 40)

Likewise Machiavelli's *The Prince* also dedicated itself to the role played by man-of-arms in the sixteenth century. Machiavelli covered not only strategy and tactics but also the political factors that influenced affairs of both war and state, such as how heads of state should govern, the moral principles of arms, dealing with dishonorable people, the difference between soldiers and mercenaries, and other subjects that the warrior scholar should have knowledge of during the sixteenth century. Machiavelli was a man of his day who fully understood the use of both sword and pen. Like Castiglione, he also realized that one was often substituted in place of the other. In writing about how a prince should keep faith with his fellow man Machiavelli stated, "You must know there are two ways of contesting, the one by the law, the other by force; the first method is proper to men, the second to beasts; but because the first is frequently not sufficient, it is necessary to have recourse to the second. Therefore it is necessary for a prince to understand how to avail himself of the beast and the man." (Machiavelli, *The Prince*, 79) Like St. Augustine, Machiavelli, as well as Castiglione, did not condemn the use of arms, they instead disapproved of their misuse.

By the turn of the fourteenth century, manuscripts that illustrated the use of weapons and unarmed methods of combat had come into being. Fiore dei Liberi's, *Flos Duellatorum*, or *Flower of Battle* was published in 1410 A.D. and conveyed its message through the use of both illustrations and verse. A master of defense himself, Fiore had first learned as a child, then as a man became well versed in the art of war. His work covered grappling, empty-handed striking, use of the dagger, pole-arms, sword and shield, fighting in armor and other areas that were crucial to battlefield combat during his day. Likewise, Hans Talhoffers'

Fechtmeister or *Fight Master* which was originally published in 1443 A.D. also covers a wide variety of combative techniques that deal with both armed and unarmed combat, and even judicial duels that were held between a man and woman. Unfortunately, in many of these early European manuscripts the artist's renditions and the words of the author were not often in sequence with one another, thus the illustrations were unable to fully portray the scope of the techniques being presented. However, the texts did provide technical data that was both sought after and useful. By the time of the Renaissance, illustrations were becoming quite comprehensive in their scope and depth. For the experienced fighter, even though the illustrated sequences might not be complete, one picture told much about a fighting art and its use. To quote Sydney Anglo,

> There are still vast gaps between what is depicted and what would have to be done in order to move from one posture to another: but it is worth making the general point here that a single picture of fencing or of wrestling usually conveys more information than an illustration of dance.
>
> —(Anglo, *The Martial Arts of Renaissance Europe*, 46)

The degree to which many of the masters of defense would go to express their ideas was considerable.

Not only did the Renaissance mindset affect the art world but those same artistic talents also illustrated various manuals written about the noble arts of defense. Even more, indicative of the Renaissance was the use of geometric and mathematical diagrams within these manuals to further illustrate footwork, strikes, attacks and defensive postures. Thus mathematics became a medium, in addition to the written word, to explore and explain the martial arts. It brought form and function to what could be considered a formless endeavor. This was especially true in the Spanish schools of fence where masters of defense like Mendoza y Quixada and Francisco Lorenz de Rada made extensive use of illustrations based on mathematical and geometric principles to define, study, and transmit knowledge pertaining to the fighting arts, particularly the art of swordsmanship. Sydney Anglo wrote about the relationship between mathematics and the fighting arts that,

> Granted this, and granted also that fencing is subordinate to mathematics, it is possible to construct a speculative and practical science in the regulation of arm and sword movements as they pass through the air in straight lines, curved lines, circles, surfaces, and spherical, cylindrical and pyramidal solids; and to regulate "the postures, dispositions, movements and operations of the body in the horizontal planes over which it may move, or subsist."
>
> —(Ibid., 87)

Despite the fact that these texts were written by skilled men-of-arms, some were appreciated more than others. While some authors pursued the technical aspects of fencing, others sought to examine the conduct and formalities that were associated with the martial arts. These observations were not always welcomed nor appreciated. In examining the Bolognese master of arms Antonio Manciolino, in 1885, English swordsman Egerton Castle, wrote in his own book *Schools and Masters of Fencing*, some two centuries after Manciolino's book had been published that, "Manciolino's text is so much filled up by wise dissertations on the rules of honour and way of picking and deciding quarrels in a gentlemanly manner, that very little actual "fencing" has found its way into his work." (Castle, *Schools and Masters of Fencing*, 34) This is despite the fact that Manciolino's work was well written and provided substantial information on sword and buckler combat, in addition to the stances, guards, and cuts used while engaged in a fight. One reason for this disapproval of Manciolino's book, may be that although informative, the book's illustrations were not related to its text and its typeface was of poor quality. It would seem that literary critics arrived almost as soon as the written word did.

The use of manuscripts and texts to present technical aspects of the fighting arts was not limited to European societies. The Japanese also made use of text and illustrations to record and transmit information about their fighting arts. *Densho* were the recorded traditions of the various *ryu* or styles of the *Koryu bujutsu*. These hand-written scrolls described not only specific techniques but also past masters, previous training routines, lists of students licensed to teach the *ryu*, and other related items considered important for maintaining the *ryu's* tradition. However, unlike many Europeans who sought to publish their written accounts and sell them to the public, the Japanese did not. They instead kept the *densho* very confidential, and these records were shown to few people and were only used by those to whom they had been rightfully passed by a system's master. Even though they could be very descriptive, just as it was with poetry and other written accounts of the fighting arts, the *densho* could also be quite cryptic and metaphoric in their presentation.

Opinions were expressed that these early texts could be used to teach those unfamiliar with the martial arts how to fight. It was a claim often made out of bravado or to bolster reputations, yet there were a handful of brave souls who did actually believe it could be done. However, combat is a very elusive endeavor where fighters seek to deceive one another, so when the untrained amateur progresses past the first illustration; then the "dance of death" remains a mystery, one which can only be unraveled by a skilled man-of-arms. Both the *densho* and European manuscripts were accounts written by men who held an in-depth knowledge of the fighting arts, and with the intended purpose of being studied seriously. Anything less would only result in confusion on the part of the casual observer and a misunderstanding of the teachings being presented. As it was with the poetry of the day, each written verse, and sometimes even the illustrations, often contained a depth of meaning that would go unnoticed unless one studied them carefully. In terms of historical perspectives, these texts and manuscripts left a means to examine early systems in detail—a godsend for the historian. The masters may or may not have been aware that words and illustrations could not fully capture the spirit and complexity of the subject on which they wrote. Their writings nevertheless provided a valuable account of not only the martial arts but also the dedicated people who practiced and wrote about them. It was these men-of-arms who were the driving force behind the development of the fighting arts.

Although many of the men who wrote these early fighting arts manuscripts were of different cultural and social backgrounds, they were not insulated from the world around them. Instead they were very much in tune with it, and recognized and understood the political, social, religious and economic forces that influenced the society in which they lived. Famed fourteenth century English poet Geoffrey Chaucer, author of the *Canterbury Tales*, wasn't just a writer, but also a man-of-arms, politician, and businessman all rolled into one uniquely gifted person. He served honorably not only on the battlefield but also in trade negotiations. He was sent to Genoa in 1372 A.D. to find a port suitable for English shipping to conduct trade with the Genoese and later he was posted as a English diplomat to Flanders and France. It was only after his duties to king and country had subsided that he began work on the *Canterbury Tales*. Likewise, there are many others in Chaucer's mold: Sir Philip Sidney, Sir Walter Raleigh, and the famed Japanese swordsman Miyamoto Musashi were all skilled with the sword and the pen. Sir Sidney, who believed in practicing with the sword everyday, composed such great works as *The Defense of Posey* and *Old Arcadia*; Musashi wrote the *Go Rin Sho* or *Book of Five Rings;* and Raleigh, who is believed to have fought more duels than any of his fellow scholar-warriors.[xix] exhibited not only his skill at verse but at the same time reflected upon his days spent on the battlefield when he wrote *Ocean to Cynthia*.

Although many who were of the commoner class could not read or write, it should not come as a surprise that those who were of the courtier or warrior class had skill in both pen and sword. Throughout history many cultures have believed that a warrior's training should comprise both martial and literary subjects. Author Stephen Pollington wrote of the English warrior poet, "Although the primary purpose of the warrior was to fight, it is no coincidence that the warrior who could use the harpstring as well as the bowstring was greatly admired." (Pollington, *The*

English Warrior, 65) In classical Greece men like Socrates and Plato were warriors as well as philosophers. Socrates himself was reputed to be without equal on campaign and during battle. He could go without food for days, march endlessly without rest, and during winter walked through snow and ice, barefoot, wearing only ordinary clothes. His attitude towards death was one of indifference and he fought as only a professional soldier could—with calculated skill and a coldness of heart.

In discussing the developmental principles behind Dr. Kano's judo, Donn Draeger explained that Kano sought to develop the "Whole Man", one who was skilled both physically and mentally. (Draeger, *Monograph 2,* 19) Long before Dr. Kano ever subscribed to this idea, classical warriors in both Europe and Asia had pursued it. Many of them sought to develop the "Whole Warrior", one skilled in both courtly and martial affairs. However, the methods used in creating verse and prose went deeper into the realms of combative applications than just those of a literary nature. This is because the same rhythms, metaphors, sequences, symbolism, and creative processes that were found within early poetry and writing could also be found in the warrior's kata and training patterns.

2-3 DANCE AND THE PROCESS OF CREATION

The use of physical based movement to transmit and record information was not unknown to the pre-modern martial artists; folk dance was a vibrant part of many early cultures. Dance has existed since pre-historic times when it was used to record past events, such as who did what during a hunt, the size of a herd of buffalo, how someone killed their prey, etc. Of all the methods used to transmit information, dance is probably the most three dimensional, for not only are physical movements used as a means to communicate, but accompanying these movements are music, song and poetry. Like the ancient Icelandic runes, which were used to record and transmit information, dance played a central role in many pagan religious ceremonies. In Okinawan society, dance has long been used as a means to transmit information, preserve legends and history, and also as a form of entertainment. George H. Kerr said of the Okinawan culture and the role dancing played in it that, "Themes for the pantomimic dance-dramas and the songs which accompanied them were drawn from legend and history, treated with a bawdy humor or tinged with melancholy, alternating between rollicking and lusty gaiety and the haunting, sad themes of separation, or poverty, or thwarted love." (Kerr, *Okinawa, The History,* 25) This proved true for not only Okinawan society, but many others as well. For the Zulu, dance served not only as a means to express themselves, but also as a form of military drill. For the ancient Greeks, war dances were used not only to exhibit individual martial prowess, but to also boost morale amongst the hoplites.

Dance has even influenced particular fighting arts. For example *pentjak-silat* has borrowed movements from Indonesian folk dances, and in turn Indonesian dancing has borrowed movements from *pentjak-silat*. In other cultures dance was also used as a means to enhance or preserve fighting techniques. The Scottish sword dance is a long and honored tradition that requires great skill and agility. Its practice develops balance, stamina, agility, and quickness in both foot and hand. Sword dances are also found in Chinese, Tibetan, Germanic, Spartan, Filipino, and African cultures.

Perhaps in no other culture's fighting arts does the intersection between poetry, song, dance, and martial technique come as close as it does in the Brazilian fighting art of *capoeira*. The system's development is largely due to African slaves who were brought to Brazil by the Portuguese to work the land. Part recreation, part fighting arts, and part art form, *capoeira* relies upon four creative mediums to express itself. Bira Almeida wrote about the system and its practice, "During the *jogo*, the *capoeiristas* explore their strengths and weaknesses, confronting their lack of knowledge, fears, and fatigue in an enjoyable, challenging, and constant process of self-improvement. The speed and attitude of the *jogo* are determined by many different rhythms of a one-string bow-shaped instrument, the *berimbau*, which is considered the symbol of capoeira." Almeida goes on to explain how the, "Singing of traditional, folkloric, and improvised songs, with clapping, enhance the energetic atmosphere and enjoyment of the rodas." (Almeida, *Capoeira,* 11) Dance not only allowed man to express himself but it also developed stamina, timing, physical agility, and preserved movements in a pre-arranged manner.[xx]

In the Filipino culture, martial forms of dance were tightly intertwined with daily life. Martial dancing was used to record battles and portray the feats of early warriors. Mark Wiley observed about the Filipino martial dances that they were broken down into three categories, or as Wiley said, "Martial dances are concerned with war and the warrior and are organized into three basic types: war or fight dances, dances which commemorate warrior of times past, and dances designed specifically for solo and paired practice of Filipino martial arts." (Wiley, *Filipino Fighting Arts,* 10) Folk dances that were used specifically in the warrior's training were known as *Langkas,* and during the performance of these dances it was not uncommon for music to be played and songs recited. Like the *Caperoia* player, the Filipinos also used music and song to enhance their fighting skills.

Although much of modern dance centers on aesthetics, it is a discipline that requires coordination, rhythm, and stamina just as the practice of a fighting art does. Dancing develops speed, focus, and timing. It employs the same muscular groups as those used by martial artists, and it is quite possible that the practice of some fighting arts kata evolved out of folk dancing. In relation to the Okinawan fighting arts, dance has been considered a process that as Matusumura *Shorin-ryu* Master Seiki Arakaki once said "softens up" the fighter's movements. Dancing aids in the development of yielding and molding actions and it was not uncommon for martial concepts and techniques to be transmitted through its practice. In discussing the similarities between Okinawan dance and karate kata, Mark Bishop author of *Okinawan Karate Teachers, Styles and Secret Techniques* wrote, "Thus as Takao Miyagi claims, it seems likely that *te* and classical dance were originally one and the same. So, for this reason, *Motobu-ryu* includes dance as part of its curriculum. In fact, the ever searching Miyagi has even gone one step further and points out that *Motobu-ryu odori-te* and classical dance can be whittled down into three distinct sets of movements:

CAPOEIRA

rising—ogami-te (prayer-hand)
reversing—coneri-te (twist-hand)
lowering—oshi-te (push-hand)"
—(Bishop, *Okinawan Karate Teachers*, 135)

Bishop even points out within his book that weapon techniques were transmitted in the same manner, and that many of
the *kobudo* katas taught within modern karate had their beginnings as dances. However, with the passage of time, the coming
of the industrialized age, and the strong impact that Japan had
on the practice of Okinawan karate during the early twentieth
century, the similarities between dance and kata became diminished in mainstream practice.[xxi] Likewise, it is quite possible that
the same had occurred within other cultures, where strong bonds
had once existed between native dance forms and their fighting
arts. The katas of a particular society's fighting art may have been
transmitted to another country, as is the case with the introduction of karate to America, but the dance forms from which the
kata evolved were not; only one half of the equation came to be
practiced. As time passed and the fighting art became more and
more naturalized within its host country, the practice of kata and

its related folkdances came to be viewed as two separate endeavors. The medium that was used by the practitioner to develop softer, more fluid movements was omitted from their training, leaving them with only hard and rigid methodologies. Interestingly enough, in reflecting upon his five decades of martial arts practice, Robert Smith wrote about well known *Shorin-ryu* practitioner, and retired Marine Corps Major Doug Cook that, "Besides his military and karate honors, Doug is in the shag dancing Hall of fame. Shag, a style of jitterbug, had its origins in the 1930's and is especially popular in the American southeast. He says that shag, in which he's won two national championships, has helped his kata enormously." (Smith, *Martial Musings*, 369) Does this mean that we all should take up dancing? It's doubtful that every fighting arts practitioner in America will do so; however, exploring the relationship between dance, poetry, and kata could prove to be of great benefit.

Although dance has existed almost as long as man has stood upright, it was only when dance intersected with man's growing martial needs that this cornerstone, upon which kata and pre-arranged training forms are built, was laid. In terms of sword dancing and other weapons, first came the weapon, then its use in combat, and finally the weapon was celebrated in dance. Eventually the same techniques used on the battlefield came to be used in dancing often with a martial tone. Dance came to be a medium for not only celebrating victories, but also for preserving and exhibiting the techniques used during battle. The rhythm, agility, and stamina developed from dancing benefited the warrior on the battlefield. This was the focal point from which so much of this world had begun.

The Process of Creation. The same creative process that led to song, poetry, language, and dance has also been used to create man's fighting arts and their pre-arranged training patterns. This resulted in similarities within man's creations. Language, song, poetry, and dance all have certain rhythms that allows one to not only execute these forms in a particular manner but to also remember them. Within kata there is a certain rhythm that aids in developing biomechanical responses, but as in poetry, it also helps the practitioner to remember the kata. Dance, poetry, language, and song all have a structured organization that gives both form and meaning to the prose or verse. Likewise, within kata there is also a structured organization that gives meaning to the techniques executed. Many poets and men of the Renaissance and Classical eras believed that words could not capture the true essence of their subject, therefore they were often used as metaphors. This is because when trying to interpret matters of a humanistic nature, the subject be so immense that it cannot be accurately described in written form, spoken word, or physical movement. These ways of communicating became symbolic of something greater than themselves. This is found within kata and forms practice, where techniques often have "layered meanings" due to the numerous possibilities that one movement can represent.

As it was with his poetry, language, and writing, man came to understand that by linking words and verses together the depth and meaning of his communication could be expanded. So to, with kata; the linking of several techniques in a pre-arranged sequence gave him a much broader and deeper base of knowledge to draw upon in the practice of his fighting arts. Most importantly, by developing kata and pre-arranged training routines, man devised a means, just as with both poetry and writing, to store and transmit martial information via a physical realm. That allowed him to reproduce information in a three dimensional way. Not only could he speak of the information, but he could also exhibit the movement or technique through physical movements. And just as it was with the written word and poetry, these movements were set in standardized sequences so that he could repeat the movements over and over again. This process allowed the warrior to not only remember specific techniques, but it also enabled him to gain proficiency in his execution thorough constant practice.

The leap of evolution that it took for man to apply the creative process that he had used in the development of literature and the arts to the combative realms was not as grand as one might think. In fact, it was a relatively small jump, if a jump at all, because all of these forms of self-expression and communication evolved in conjunction with one another. At the same time that prehistoric man was developing the spear he was also learning how to talk. When great Greek minds like Plato, Socrates, and Aristotle established Western philosophy, they also laid the foundations of Western warfare. Although poetry, language, and dance are different endeavors, the process used to create them is one and the same; thus, Plato could talk of philosophy and fighting within the context of a solitary sentence. In fact, it was the Greek mathematician Pythagoras who sought to prove that all things were related through numbers. Although he believed that man's world was revealed to him by intellect and not intuition, Pythagoras still sought out the fundamental similarities between all things that to him were linked by numeric equations. As Bertrand Russell wrote about Pythagoras and his quest, "He discovered the importance of numbers in music, and the connection which he established between music and arithmetic survives in the mathematical terms 'harmonic mean' and 'harmonic progression.' He thought of numbers as shapes, as they appear on dice or playing cards. We still speak of squares and cubes of numbers, which are terms that we owe to him." (Russell, *History of Western Philosophy,* 35) The numeric relationships that Pythagoras used to interpret his world can also be used to explain physical and spiritual similarities that are found within the fighting arts and how they relate to other rituals found within a society.

The Zen state of mind can be experienced through both kata and tea ceremonies, as well as meditation and painting. Likewise, the cultivation of *Qi* can be performed through both hard and soft systems of martial arts; in Chinese fighting arts this is accomplished in both *Shaolin* and *taijiquan*, Okinawan *karate-ka* through the practice of *Sanchin*. Nor is the cultivation of Zen and *Qi* limited to the Asian combatives; *capoeira* players believe that "*Ache*" or the force of life that all living things have can be cultivated through the practice of *capoeira,* and they utilize specific rituals and movements to accomplish this goal.

By examining Pythagoras and his numeric theory we come to understand that man's creative process is not just regulated to

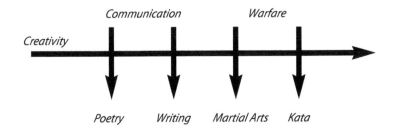

solitary events, but instead is applied to everything within his world. When the need for meaning intersects with his creative powers, a new form of expression evolves, be it kata, poetry, art, speech etc.[xxii] As Karen Armstrong wrote about experience when related to religion and matters of a spiritual nature, "The vision came from the heart and the affections rather than what Wordsworth called the 'meddling intellect' whose purely analytic powers could destroy this kind of intuition. People did not need learned books and theories. All that was required was a 'wise passiveness' and 'a heart that watches and receives.' Insight began with a subjective experience, although this had to be 'wise,' not uninformed and self-indulgent." (Armstrong, *A History of God,* 348) When reading Armstrong's statement it is no small wonder why many early people considered the poet and the warrior to be empowered and inspired by a divine force, since they brought form to something almost indescribable: a realm of the human experience that existed but could not be seen save in its aftermath. The poet took verse and gave both form and meaning to the world around him, while the warrior devised established techniques, principles, and philosophies that gave form to the art of war.

The above illustration demonstrates the creative process involved when man's needs and creative instincts intersect. The horizontal line represents man's creative powers. The vertical lines that intersect with it represent his needs or external forces, such as communication and warfare. The bottom represents the creations that result from when the two forces intersect, which in this case are poetry, writing, martial arts, and the practice of kata.

The surge or path of the human creative spirit is constant and thriving; in fact it is one of the forces that have sustained mankind's survival. The path of creativity is unbroken, yet often intersected by different needs or external forces present in the environment. However, in each case, it is the same creative and intellectual process used to solve these problems, therefore, in many of the resulting creations there are similarities to be found. For a creation to be born, it takes both the object, upon which man's creative powers are focused, and his creativity for the experience to be complete. As Kenneth Yasuda wrote about *haiku*, "Without a significant object there can be no aesthetic experience," without it, a *haiku* becomes, in Yamamoto's words, "A mere proverb. A *haiku* comes into being through inspiration arising from a special object meaningful to the poet. If such a special object...is lost from view, the *haiku* becomes akin to a mere proverb." (Yasuda, *The Japanese Haiku,* 49) So true are his words that they apply to not only *haiku* but also to warfare. Although combat is not the aesthetic experience of *haiku*, when man focuses his creative powers on the "significant object" of warfare, then the martial arts and their kata come into being. As he gave form to his world, and sought to explain the mysteries of life through the creation of mythology, religion, science, mathematics, art, and philosophy, man also described combat. He gave it form through a creative process, that allowed him to understand the complexities of combat in human terms. This process was not an option for mankind, but a necessity for his continued survival, for of all the crucibles encountered, warfare has proven to be the most demanding. In combat the warrior has to maintain control over his own physical and mental state, as well as contend with the murderous intentions of the enemy. The experience tests man on every level of his existence: physical, mental, spiritual, and even ethical considerations are all touched by the hand of combat. To understand, perfect his skills, and survive warfare, man gave it form through established rituals such as kata and systematic methods of fighting.

The art of war is a structured creation. It is neither the aesthetic structure of poetry, nor the orderly method of writing one finds instead a structure in which both form and chaos exist side-by-side, each complementing the other. No matter how hard the warrior seeks to control the battlefield and bring order to its death and mayhem, there will always be chaos, and it is for this experience that he has to prepare the most. The warrior must have the ability to act intuitively, to have faith in himself, and—at the very moment of crisis—rely upon his natural rhythms and instincts that come from his heart and not the meddling intellect of which Wordsworth wrote. No matter how advanced man's creative powers or intellect may be, at the very heart of warfare's blood-filled cauldrons, chaos always rules supreme.

CHAPTER 3

The Spur of Development: Combat

When war is reduced to its simplest elements, we find that there are only two ways in which an enemy can be met and defeated. Either the shock or the missile must be employed against him.

—Sir Charles Oman, 1885

Although martial arts originated from the intersection between war and creativity, it was on the field of battle that the birth of kata took place. The catalog of battle-tested techniques was made out of necessity. Sir Richard Burton stated about their relationships that, "Painting and sculpture were the few simple lines drawn and cut upon the tomahawk or other rude weapon-tool. 'As men think and live so they built,' said Herder; and the architecture, which presently came to embrace all other arts, dawned when the Savage attempted to defend and to adorn his roost among the tree branches or the entrance to his cave den."

(Burton, *Book of the Sword,*15) As he learned to transmit and preserve other knowledge, early man realized that the same had to be done with techniques and tactics that had proven themselves effective during the hunt or on the field of battle. He began to record specific techniques in pre-arranged sequences. These proved to be very effective in preserving and transmitting of combative techniques and would later be the foundation on which many martial systems would be built.

Man's earliest attempts at creating training patterns and codifying prescribed techniques were no doubt very rudimentary, like his early poetry. However, as time passed and his martial skills grew in sophistication, so did his kata. There were many factors that contributed to this process and not all of them had the same intent. Although combat is the spur of development for both the fighting arts and their kata, combat varies according to the social, geographical, political, and cultural forces at work. For the sixteenth century knight, the idea of kicking their opponent in the face as a means of fighting wasn't contemplated. This is because of their social attitudes and the fact that they were armed with a sword most of the time. There was no need to kick an opponent because a sword was a more effective means of disposal, not to mention the fact that they wore armor during battle, that would have prohibited them from executing such a technique. For the eighteenth century Frenchman engaged in a duel, thrusting one's *epee* into an antagonist's chest was proper form; yet had the same technique and weapon been used two hundred years earlier, it would have had little or no effect. This is because the sixteenth century knight fought his battles dressed from head to foot in body armor, and a mere thrust executed with a light *epee* would not have penetrated his chest piece. However, for the eighteenth century *capoeira* player living in Rio de Janeiro, the idea of kicking their opponent in the head was perfectly acceptable and an often performed technique. The *capoeira* player was not allowed to carry a sword, therefore, he relied heavily upon his hands and feet for defense. The premodern man-of-arms used a wide variety of weapons under different circumstances.

Differences in the social, geographical, cultural, and historical periods were reflected in the kata and pre-arranged training patterns used. The sixteenth century samurai understood that some sword cuts could be performed against particular areas of an armored foe, while others could not. To stab into the foe's mid-section with was safe and effective. Enemies would stop dead in their tracks. However, cutting the wrist as the enemy's downward cut was being performed would achieve nothing because the arm's downward motion would continue despite the fact that the hand had been severed. These "lessons" learned thorough trial and error on the battlefield were incorporated into the samurai's kata.

It was not just the samurai who understood these bio-mechanical reactions. Egerton Castle observed about seventeenth and eighteenth century prize fighters that, "It is difficult to understand how men could pass through many ordeals, and yet remain physically fit to handle a sword with vigor and dexterity. But such was evidently the case, showing how little dangerous, after all, mere cutting of muscles is to strong and healthy men—a single puncture with a small sword through the lungs or abdomen would probably have settled these sturdy gladiators for life." (Castle, *Schools and Masters of Fencing,* 203) His words reflect upon not only the differences found between prize fighting and mortal combat, but also the different techniques and their effects. Written observations made by Castle and others were stored and practiced in the pre-arranged training sequences.

These sequences or kata were more than just random movements linked together. Each pre-arranged sequence and the techniques found within it took on a meaning of their own. The performance of these pre-arranged sequences reflected lessons learned that dealt with not only physical concepts, but the state of mind as well. Through constant practice a behavioral pattern was developed in which the techniques in the kata were executed unconsciously. Each pre-arranged sequence was in essence, a living, breathing entity that encompassed the physical and mental realms of development.

Long before the development of kata there was warfare, and it was in this "classroom" that many warriors learned their lessons. The warrior of Western or Eastern culture was not born with a martial prowess, but had to learn it. It was only after the warrior had learned his lessons that he began to record them—and not vice versa. His kata were the acquired skills he found the most effective, and by recording them the warrior enabled himself to further perfect these skills and transmit them to others.

Often the classical kata were based on two-person interactions, where one would act as the attacker and the other as the defender. These methods were viewed differently than the methods of today. Whereas modern kata practice is often done for spiritual development or competition, the earlier forms were practiced to preserve and transmit information. The concept of kata practice as a means for spiritual enlightenment was considered secondary by the thirteenth century samurai, Viking, or Renaissance swordsman. Despite the other benefits gained from kata practice, these early men-of-arms' primary concerns were the perfect transmission of effective techniques. Kata were teaching/training methods by which successful techniques were preserved and passed on. These pre-arranged scenarios were never intended as an end to themselves and, in fact, a caution against viewing kata as a training goal was made by Yagyu Munenori in his *Heiho Kadensho* when he states, 'Learn well all of the above (various kata of *Shinkage-ryu*) and from them devise thousands of new maneuvers. After mastering the way (of the *Shinkage-ryu*), one should not speak of such things as 'numbers of sword techniques.'" (Hall, *Hoplos,* Winter 1989)

Classical kata were much the same as the firing range is to the modern day infantryman who goes to the rifle range to perfect his marksmanship in anticipation of using it on the battlefield. His practice requires concentration, dexterity, and control of his weapon, but the soldier does not look upon the experience as anything more than perfecting his marksmanship. The postures used in shooting may be combined or modified during combat to suit the needs of his environment; he will not bind himself to using a prone or kneeling position to fire from. Although used frequently on the firing range, these positions, just as the techniques used within kata, are examples of how the weapon *can* be fired, not the only way that it *should* be fired.

Steps in the Process of Kata Development
1. *Development of specific weapon.*
2. *Use of weapon in combat or hunting.*
3. *Evaluation of specific techniques.*
4. *Continual use of specific techniques.*
5. *Identification of specific techniques.*
6. *Assimilation of specific techniques in a pre-arranged form (includes folkdance).*
7. *Practice of specific techniques in pre-arranged order.*
8. *Transmission of techniques from one person to another through pre-arranged form.*

Pre-arranged forms of training evolved from three basic methods of fighting: military, civilian, and sport. All three of these combative realms use pre-arranged training to preserve and transmit techniques and to develop bio-mechanical responses through repetitive practice. Those kata that were developed for use in the military were influenced by battlefield combat. They included the use of spears, bow and arrows, swords, glaives, body armor, and shields. These methods were offensive in nature. The kata forms of the civilian realm were not as concerned with battlefield combat as they were with self-defense and duels of honor. These forms relied on empty handed methods of fighting as seen with karate or weapons such as walking staffs, small swords, rapiers, and *epees*. Combative sports have as long and distinguished a history as the battlefield and civilian fighting arts. With the evolution of weapons and systems used in war and civil affairs, there also came the evolution of combative sports. From the early Cretan society and Japanese sumo wrestling's roots, to the prize fights of seventeenth and eighteenth century Europe, combative sports have been practiced by most cultures with an established martial tradition. All three of the methodologies have influenced and impacted the formation and practice of kata training. The following will examine each method, its weapons and characteristics and why they were used extensively by early men-of-arms.

3-1 MILITARY SYSTEMS

Much of how a society's art of war evolved is due to its interaction with other cultures; hence, it can be stated that advanced societies also have advanced martial arts.

Arms and armor have always played a major role in battlefield combat, and as societies advanced so did their weaponry. Our Paleolithic and Neolithic forefathers made use of sticks and rocks for weapons, the hand-stone being the preferred weapon of choice. Flint, which is easy to chip into a sharpened edge, was one of the most sought-after materials for making weapons. Man's first attempts to make weaponry were not for warfare, but to defend himself against the wild animals who hunted him or for killing game for food. As time passed and mankind's means to produce arms advanced, he developed more sophisticated weapons such as spears, axes, and knives, which often were manufactured from flint or stone. During pre-historic times man realized that there was greater power in numbers, consequently he began to band together into tribal societies. This led to the development of agricultural techniques, the clearing of land, the building of roads, stone structures, monuments and temples, as well as trade between different tribes. With this breakup into groups there also came disputes over territory, crops, water and other matters crucial to survival. It was not long after before warfare came into being and man began using his hunting weapons to fight other humans.

Warfare was initially a crude affair with two opposing tribes facing off in battlelines tossing spears and rocks, shooting arrows at one another, and exchanging shouts and insults. Some tribe members would become brave enough to cross the no-mans land separating the two sides in an attempt to thrust their wooden spear into the belly of a foe. Usually these ritualized wars would last for a few hours, or until sunset, then both parties would leave the field, often without a clear resolution.

Man's ability to produce food enabled him to plant and harvest crops. He was able to store surplus food and in doing so took up permanent residence on the land he farmed. This led to organized societies with structured levels of government and an easier lifestyle, which at the same time, caused more difficulties since others would try to take his fertile crop lands. The warrior class arose to meet these new threats. Since he no longer lived hand to mouth, man now had time to devote to the art of war, and this in time would provide a stimulus for other advances in both weaponry and tools. As his means to make both war and weapons advanced, crude body armor was worn on the battlefield, shields came to be used, and even organized techniques and tactics were employed. By the time of the rise of organized governments and city states, both man's weapons and his means to use them had evolved. As the city state grew in power so did its ways of war: fortifications, catapults, naval forces, chariots, incineration type weapons, and organized systems of martial arts all came to be used.

Examining the early city states and their martial arts, is like going back in time. Ewart Oakeshott wrote about the study of arms and the fighting arts in his classic study, *The Archaeology of Weapons* that, "In dealing with the development of arms and the art of war, it seems to be customary to begin at the period of time long before Rome itself began. At some time about 1900 B.C. certain events completely changed the warlike outlook of all peoples of the ancient East and destroyed those who (like the peaceable people of the Indus civilization of Mohenjo Daro) had none." (Oakeshott, *The Archaeology of Weapons,* 15) Oakeshott's writing reflects much on the organized history of the battlefield fighting arts that were in existence long before the Roman Empire. And indeed by 1900 B.C., the Indo-European peoples had conquered vast territories through the use of chariots, spears, and swords. However, they were not the only ones to do so, as the societies of the Asian continent also have long and distinguished martial heritages. One example is India, whose Tamil martial traditions can be traced back to at least 4 B.C., and China's martial history is some 5,000 years old. An integral part of both of these cultures' martial traditions, with many other cultures, is the use of organized weapons systems. Some of the earliest recordings of advanced weapons manufacture and their use in China are from the time of the "Yellow Emperor" (2690-2590 B.C) when weapons were made of jade, copper, and gold. Dr.

Yang, Jwing-Ming wrote about this era in Chinese history that: "Not until the time of the first recorded emperor, Huang Di (2690-2590 B.C), does evidence exist for advanced weapons made of material other than stone. Huang Di, called the "Yellow Emperor" because he occupied the territory near the Yellow River, had weapons made of jade, copper, and gold. This period, therefore, traditionally marks the beginning of the metallurgical sciences in arms manufacturing in China." (Yang, *Ancient Chinese Weapons,* 10) The same process that Dr. Yang describes occurred in other societies, and with advances in metallurgical techniques the quality of both man's weapons and war fighting skills improved.

Ironic as it may seem, our ancestors' discovery of pottery led to the development of more efficient weapons and fighting arts. Prior to the making of pottery, the early use of fire was as an open flame on which meals were cooked and people took refuge from the elements by its warmth. However, with the development of pottery around 5000 B.C., man began to enclose his fires into crude kilns to increase the temperature of the firing. This allowed him to not only produce hardened pottery, but this new technology also gave him the ability to melt copper and shape it into various forms such as edged weapons. Some 1,500 years later, he discovered that by melting both copper and tin together, a harder metal was forged called bronze. With the discovery and development of bronze came better weapons and body armor. Another leap in metallurgy was to take place around 1500 B.C. with the discovery of iron. Through his own creative process and intellect, man learned that with a higher heat source he could separate iron from the ore, which was widespread and easily obtained. This discovery was a significant advance in his weaponry and life, and with it came the Iron Age.

With the development of metal weapons and man's appreciation for them, his martial horizons broadened considerably. With the sharpened metal edge, not only could he strike as was done before, but now he could cut and stab in a much more lethal manner with a weapon far more durable than those before. This advantage was particularly profound with the discovery of iron, which proved to be a substance far superior to copper or bronze. The weapons made from it gave the warrior a great advantage on the battlefield. From this advance in technology, new techniques and martial applications arose. With time's passage and the spread of copper, then bronze, and finally iron-forging technology, man began to manufacture metal-edged weapons. Yet it was not just metal forging that gave rise to different techniques and styles of fighting. Different body types, cultural surroundings, and particular styles of warfare also influenced this portion of the martial evolutionary cycle. It was these factors, along with metal smithing technologies, that caused a multitude of techniques to come into being from a variety of weapons and armor.

From the development of man's weapons, systems to use them came to be. First came the weapon and with time and trial and error, came the systematic means to use the weapon, followed by a system's pre-arranged methods of training. And although weapons systems and their respective martial arts styles evolved in many different societies, and at various times in history, there are fundamental similarities to be found within all of them. Consider the sixteenth century Japanese samurai who is executes his downward cut with a *katana*, and the fifteenth century German man-of-arms who does the same using a two handed sword. Both warrior's techniques will follow a similar trajectory due to the structure of the human body. The chopping motion used by the Roman soldier with his *gladius* is the same one employed by the modern *bando* player with his *kukri*. The body armor worn by the Roman soldier in 54 B.C. had the same purpose and many of the same components as that worn by the sixteenth century Japanese samurai. These similarities are found within kata and pre-arranged training patterns.[xxiii] There are three basic categories that the warrior's hand-held weapons can be segmented into. They are:

1. Pole-arms, such as spears, *naginatas*, glaives, halberds, maces, etc.
2. Short arms such as swords, axes and knives.
3. Empty-handed methods of combat.

All three of these categories have played an integral part in the warrior's survival on the battlefield. Despite the differences found in each category of weapon and system, they were viewed as parts of a whole. For the classical man-of-arms, proficiency in all three categories was a requirement for his survival; he was not a specialist, but instead a generalist well versed in all forms of combat. Combatants used a blend of tactics that are now considered individual systems.

One did not engage in combat with just one weapon, but with several. When the great explorer Ferdinand Magellan met his death in battle against Filipino tribesmen in 1521 A.D., he fought, as did the rest of his men with pike and sword, while others used firearms and crossbows; cannons mounted on boats stationed offshore supported his whole landing party. His Filipino adversaries also fought in a similar manner using bolo knives, spears, and even rocks. Neither side's warriors restricted themselves to just one weapon. Contrary to popular belief, the spear wreaked great havoc on both sides during the battle. Tim Joyner wrote about the combat and Magellan's death,

> Lapulapu's forces attacked with redoubled fury, aiming their spears and poisoned arrows at the unprotected legs of the retreating Spaniards. One of the poisoned arrows grazed Magellan's leg, and yet another mortally wounded Cristovao Rebel, who had been fighting valiantly alongside his father. When Magellan saw that the young man had been killed, he went berserk and hurled himself at the enemy, getting so far ahead of his defenders that they were unable to protect him. Surrounded by the enemy, he was pelted furiously with stones that knocked off his helmet. A defending warrior slashed his leg with a bolo and he fell helpless to the ground. Bamboo spears were thrust into his body wherever it was unprotected by armor. A spear through the throat was the coup de grace."
> —Joyner, *Magellan*, 195)

Joyner's account is a prime example of how men employed a number of weapons during combat, relying on each one as a specific need arose.[xxiv] The different systems associated with each weapon evolved within their own channels, and each weapon held its own distinctive traits that influenced the transaction of combat.

The following provides examples of the weapons found within each category and their use in combat.

Pole-arms. Man learned that killing from a distance was safer than in close proximity to his foe or prey. The closer he was to his enemies the better the chance they had of hurting him. One of the first weapons used to fill the gap between man and foe was the club, followed by the sharpened stick, which was in time destined to become the spear. These basic weapons were two-thirds of the foundation for the evolution of pole-arms. The other third of the equation came when man first tied flint knives to the end of his club or long stick. This allowed him not only to stab but also to cut and slash. He could kill at a distance from his prey or foe, and by doing so limit their ability to retaliate. Another benefit was soon discovered: the weapon's length bestows its user with a psychological advantage—the trauma of combat is reduced. The closer you are to your enemy the more personal the act becomes, thus the greater the fear level from the increased chances of an enemy wounding or killing you. However, there is another factor involved, and that is the fact that distance allows a de-humanization process to occur, that makes the act of killing easier. Lt. Col. Dave Grossman wrote about distance's effect on combat and the use of arms, "First we must recognize that it is psychologically easier to kill with an edged weapon that permits a long stand-off range, and increasingly more difficult as the stand-off range decreases. Thus it is considerably easier to impale a man with a twenty-foot pike than it is to stab him with a six-inch knife." (Grossman, *Killing the Psychological Cost of Killing*, 120)

Even in pre-modern times, psychological factors were taken into consideration. For those warriors welding pole-arms, not only did the long weapon make it easier to kill their opponent, but also to have the courage to face their enemy.[xxv] Withstanding the charge of heavy cavalry was a major concern for the foot soldier, both physically and mentally. The charge of heavy horses and mounted men was a fierce and deadly vision that caused many warriors to turn and flee, only to be slaughtered as they tried to outrun the horses' charge. However, with the use of pole arms (i.e. spears), the length of the weapon allowed the warrior a safety zone that put enough distance between him and his enemy so that he could stand and fight effectively. Likewise the man armed with a pole-arm who fought an opponent armed with a sword, had an increased chance of survival. In fact, the pole-arm usually proved to be the better weapon when pitted against a sword. In 1625 A.D. Richard Peeke, a British sailor, was captured by Spanish musketeers and then interrogated. During his questioning, Peeke was asked if he thought they were a match for the British. Out of national pride, Peeke challenged his captors to a fight and he soon found himself facing three Spaniards all armed with rapiers and daggers. Armed only with a quarterstaff, Peeke killed one of the swordsmen outright and seriously injured the other two. The Spanish were so impressed that they set him free. (Brown, *English Martial Arts,* 69) The use of the pole-arm grew and as techniques, tactics, and styles of fighting evolved. The classification of pole-arms can be broken down into three basic categories they are: spears, halberds, and war clubs. The use of all three of these weapons is found in many cultures, they were not limited to one society, time, or place in the history of warfare.

Spears. Although swords are usually associated with the aristocratic class and military elite, spears, lances, and pole-arms were also used extensively by the nobility and all classes of man. For the peoples of Northwestern and Central Africa the spear and sword "are the only manly and becoming weapons." (Burton, *Book of the Sword,* 162) The spear's use in combat was widespread, from foot soldiers in wedge formations to knights mounted atop horses; it has been even used from the backs of chariots and elephants. Among the Chinese, the spear was considered the supreme long weapon due to its versatility. As Dr. Yang Jwing-Ming wrote, "The spear is called 'king of the long weapons' because its techniques are superior to those of other weapons." (Yang, *Ancient Chinese Weapons,* 24) Some of the most noted warriors to use this weapon were the Celtic Gaesatae, who went into battle naked and armed only with a spear. The

Gaesatae fought naked in observance of an ancient belief system that nudity would give them supernatural protection against their enemies. (Chadwick, *The Celts,* 134) Others also employed the spear in battle. The Greeks used it extensively in their fighting arts as did the Japanese, Koreans, Burmese, Native Americans, and a host of other cultures. Although there are many variations to its design, one thing remains constant: its sharp point mounted at the end of a long piece of wood, which gives the warrior the ability to engage their opponents far beyond arm's length.

Halberd. The halberd, like the spear, is found within many cultures' fighting arts and was also used extensively on the battlefield. Although often associated with Japanese martial arts due to the popularity of the *Naginata*, this style of weapon was also used in European martial arts. At the battle of Morgarten in 1315 A.D., a force of 3,000 Swiss infantry armed with halberds ambushed and slaughtered an invading force of Austrians, many of whom were knights. Kelly DeVries wrote about the Swiss and their halberds; "Using their famed 'halberds', the Swiss easily cut down most of the knights from their horses, killing them as they lay helpless on the ground." (DeVries, *Infantry Warfare,* 189) Likewise, the English "Bill" was a great favorite among that country's men-of-arms. During an inventory of arms at the tower of London in 1547 A.D. there were over 7,000 Bills counted in the armory's inventory. (Brown, *English Martial Arts,* 72)

The halberd style of pole-arm is a long, sharpened blade attached to the end of a rod or long piece of wood. Like the spear, it can be used to stab, but with its sharp blade it is also employed to cut, and when used this way the results very often proved devastating. In some instances, the weapon was used to break up cavalry charges by cutting the legs from beneath the enemy's horses. For the samurai, the *Naginata* was one of their favorite weapons and could be wielded either on horseback or on foot. Its use required great skill and stamina, and the weapon itself was very versatile, allowing its exponent to use its blade, butt, and even shaft during combat. Over 400 of the *Bujutsu ryu-ha* had the *nagainata* in their teachings.

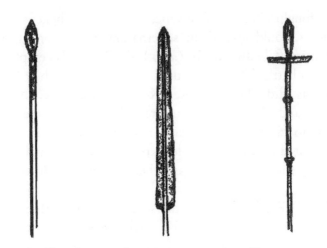

SPEARS FROM THREE CULTURES—SWISS FIFTEENTH CENTURY PIKE, MASAI SPEAR HEAD, JAPANESE WINGED SPEAR

Clubs. Perhaps one of the oldest, yet easiest pole-arms to wield is the club. Man's first pole-arm and the easiest to manufacture, the club has a long and distinguished history in the fighting arts of many cultures. From the Native Americans to the Maoris of New Zealand, and both the European and Asian martial arts, clubs have been used on the battlefield and have had codified techniques established for their use. During the fifteenth century in Europe, war clubs and maces took on stylistic designs; they were often adorned in much the same finery as swords. The shafts of maces and war clubs were made from either wood or metal, and in the hands of a skilled warrior proved to be very deadly weapons. The length of these weapons often depended upon the user's own taste. Some could be three feet or less, while others could range up to six feet or more. In some instances where the weapon was one of large frame, like the Japanese *tetsubo*, which was a large metal rod with spikes on its sides, it required a strong person due to its size and weight. These factors also limited its movement patterns. Therefore, timing became critical in the employment of the weapon on the battlefield—its user had to know exactly when to strike, for if not executed properly the person wielding the *tetsubo* would be left with an opening in his defenses. In other instances such as with smaller maces, the weapon could be used by the average man-of-arms and

FIFTEENTH CENTURY SWISS HALBERD (TOP), JAPANESE NAGINATA (BOTTOM)

employed with a wide range of movement. Its techniques were similar to those of the sword, with the mace being used in hacking and slashing motions as well as thrusting. The weapon was also used as a training device to enhance swords skills. Alfred Hutton wrote of its use in seventeenth century London prize playing that; "The cudgel, too, must not be lost sight of; it was used, and is so still, as a means for studying the art of the broadsword." (Hutton, *The Sword and the Centuries,* 287)

Although the club's use was overshadowed by other weapons and their methods, it still proved to be a very effective weapon despite its simple design. The same held true with staff weapons, which were often considered a peasant's weapon, but nonetheless were used with lethal effect on many battlefields. The use of pole-arms has always been included in martial arts systems. Even today within many modern militaries, the bayonet is still issued and practiced, though its use in combat has been reduced drastically due to high technology weaponry. Nonetheless, the tradition of the pole-arm, which began when our pre-historic ancestors first picked up a stick to defend themselves, still lives on.

Swords and Empty Hands. Perhaps no other weapon known to man has captured his imagination so much as the sword. The weapon has often been a symbol for the duality of our world, for with its sharp edge the sword can sustain all things good and cut away all things evil; it can both save and take life. D.T. Suzuki wrote about it that: "The sword comes to be identified with the annihilation of things that lie in the way of peace, justice, progress, and humanity. It stands for all that is desirable for the spiritual welfare of the world at large. It is now the embodiment of life and not death." (Suzuki, *Zen and Japanese Culture*, 89) Man has associated he sword with such traits as honor, integrity, and courage, and it has been both feared and worshipped within our world and found throughout history in battle, myth, and religion.

Of all the warrior's weapons, the sword was the most difficult to develop. The sword is not a primitive weapon easily chipped from flint like a knife or arrowhead, nor is it made by sharpening the end of a stick, as are the primitive spear and javelin. To make the sword requires knowledge of metallurgy. Although flint knives, spears, and axes had been developed early, these weapons were limited in their size, flint being so brittle a material. Likewise, wooden swords were manufactured and used by early cultures but their blades amounted to not much more than clubs with fine points. Though effective, they still lacked the ability to cut and puncture. The development of the sword and its sharpened edge gave man the ability to not only cut, thrust, and kill, but also a means to conquer other lands. Even though earlier swords may look crude in design, their function use and role in warfare remained almost unchanged for 3,000 years.

Ewart Oakeshott wrote about the sword and its use throughout the ages, "The Stone Age men fought with axe and spear, for the sword was never a primitive weapon: its earliest forms were as sophisticated and as elegant as its latest—the middle Bronze Age joins hands across thirty centuries with the court of Louis XV." (Oakeshott, *The Archaeology of Weapons*, 24-25) Indeed, the earliest bronze rapier's thrust would prove to be just as fatal as one performed by a seventeenth century duelist with his small sword. Both men would execute their thrusts in a similar, if not the same manner.

Although the dagger has been used since the beginning of the Bronze Age (3100 B.C), many people believe some of the first

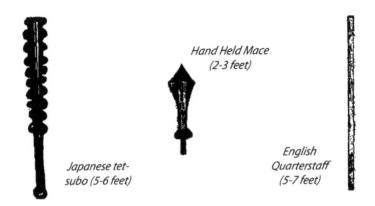

Hand Held Mace (2-3 feet)

Japanese tetsubo (5-6 feet)

English Quarterstaff (5-7 feet)

JAPANESE TETSUBO, HAND HELD MACE, ENGLISH QUARTERSTAFF

swords were developed in Minoan Crete around the year 1500 B.C. (Ibid, 25). As man sharpened his bronze knife he noticed that it began to change form; its blade became suitable for both thrusting and cutting. Over time he began to experiment with his dagger trying to improve its design, which gradually led to longer and sturdier blades being made. This process of development continued. By the middle of the Bronze Age not only had man developed a suitable blade, but also an improved hilt that would not break so easily upon impact. This allowed him to use his sword more freely on the battlefield, and before long this new technology spread to where other people were making swords. In China, some of the earliest swords were manufactured around the time of Huang Di, who was the first recorded emperor of China. Likewise, in Japan there is evidence of swords being used as early as 200 B.C.

The diffusion of sword-making technology, just as with other forms of technical expertise, spread rapidly from those points where it originated. Its adaptation and assimilation was affected by geographical regions. For those people who lived in very remote areas, where there was little interaction between them and other societies, the possibility of assimilating sword-smith and metallurgy techniques would prove very remote. For others who lived in areas where commerce and interaction with surrounding societies was commonplace, the adaptation of sword-

TWO VERSIONS OF EARLY FLINT KNIVES USED FOR HUNTING AND WARFARE. THEIR SHAPES WERE OBTAINED BY TAKING A ROCK AND CHIPPING AT A PIECE OF FLINT UNTIL THE DESIRED TOOL OR WEAPON WAS MADE.

smith techniques was very probable. Jared Diamond wrote, "The societies most accessible to receiving inventions by diffusion were those embedded in major continents. In these societies technology developed most rapidly, because they accumulated not only their own inventions but also those of other societies. For example medieval Islam, centrally located in Eurasia, acquired inventions from India and China and ancient Greek learning." (Diamond, *Guns, Germs and Steel,* 257) This method of migration would have much effect on the development of and practice of martial arts, especially when firearm technology became abundant. However, even prior to the spread of firearms, the effects of this transfer of technology were felt and noted. For those who fought with stone or even bronze weapons against others armed with iron, the results could prove devastating. Likewise, for those armed only with wooden clubs and flint knives against an enemy armed with sword and spear, the battle's outcome most assuredly was in favor of the swordsman. Thus, advanced societies accumulated and developed advanced weapons and martial arts.

Cut Thrust-Primary and Secondary Uses. In examining the sword and its use, there are two basic but very relevant arguments about the use of this weapon. Both are reflected in the kata and training routines associated with the sword. The two points of dispute are: 1) Is the sword a secondary or primary weapon? 2)

NEPALESE KUKRI (LEFT). PRIMARILY A CUTTING BLADE, ONE USED EXTENSIVELY BY THE GURKHAS. DOUBLE EDGED VIKING SWORD (RIGHT) OF THE TENTH CENTURY. THIS WEAPON CAN BE USED TO EITHER CUT OR THRUST. THE VIKINGS WERE ACCOMPLISHED METALSMITHS AND THIS WAS REFLECTED IN THEIR SWORDS, WHICH WERE MADE BY SKILLED CRAFTSMEN WHO WOULD RICHLY DECORATE WEAPONS.

Which way is it better to use the sword, to cut or thrust? Much of this dispute depends on the type of sword and the time and place it was used during the long history of warfare. The Roman soldier and English knight exemplify the sword's use as a primary and secondary weapon. For the Roman soldier, his *gladius* and shield were his primary weapons. As the Roman Empire grew, so to did its martial arts. Originally its men-of-arms blundered along in an uncoordinated manner, but by 50 A.D. their methods of war had become very sophisticated. No longer did the soldiers advance as a mob but instead walking silently across the battlefield in a very coordinated and controlled formation. Before reaching his enemy the Roman soldier would throw his *pilum*, which was a specially designed javelin that was intended to penetrate the enemies' shields and make them useless. Next, the Roman soldier would close with his foe in order to allow him to use his sword and shield in close-quarter combat. As Adrian Goldsworthy wrote, "Roman doctrine emphasized individual aggression, and soldiers were taught to get close to their opponent in order to use their short-bladed *gladii*. The standard drill was to punch the enemy in the face with the shield-boss and then stab him in the stomach." (Goldsworthy, *Roman Warfare*, 125) Their shields were very heavy and could produce a good deal of damage, while a thrust to the abdomen with the *gladii,* or short sword, would most certainly result in a very agonizing death. The *gladius* itself could be used to either cut or thrust, but its redeeming quality was its size. The weapon's blade was not much over two feet long, and this allowed for its use at close quarters where larger swords could not be used. Julius Caesar, in his first hand account of the Gallic wars, gives a very good example of the Roman soldier's use of the *pilum* and *gladius* when he wrote about one battle his men fought against the Helvetii,

> The legionaries, with the advantage of higher ground, easily smashed the enemy's formation with a volley of pikes, and having thus thrown it into confusion drew their swords and charged. The Gallic line was now in serious difficulties: our pikes had in many cases pierced through several shields at once and locked them together. The iron had bent, and they could neither withdraw it nor fight properly with the left arm thus engaged. Many of them tried for some time to shake themselves free, but in the end preferred to drop their shields and fight with no body protection.
> —(Caesar, *The Gallic Wars,* 18)

Those tribesmen who dropped their shields and fought, were at a disadvantage; for even though the Romans were outnumbered, their skill with sword and shield drove the Gallic tribesmen from the battlefield.

Although the sword is the weapon most commonly associated with the European Medieval and Renaissance martial arts, in many instances it was secondary to the spear, halberd, and other pole-arms whose use on the battlefield was a long and continued many successes. The lance was used extensively by the knights of the Renaissance and Medieval eras, and before the sword was employed in battle it was the lance that opened most combats. The sword could only be used after the action had closed to a distance to where the lance's length made it impractical to use. It was not uncommon, though, for the knight's lance to be modified for him to use at close quarters. For instance, at the battle of Poitiers in 1356 A.D. French knights, fighting on foot, cut down their lances to six feet in length to be able to use them unmounted and at close range. Sydney Anglo wrote about the use of pole-arms favored over the sword, "Yet, despite their diversity and widespread use, staff weapons never received anything like the volume of literary attention which masters of arms bestowed upon the sword—just as they have rarely aroused much interest among historians." (Anglo, *The Martial Arts of Renaissance Europe*, 148) This is very true within the annals of martial history, from both the European and Asian traditions where most attention is focused upon the sword. Although not strangers to using the sword, the Greeks also looked upon it as a secondary weapon. For the hoplite his spear was the preferred weapon on the battlefield; however, when he found himself at close quarters where his spear could not be employed he fought with his *kopis*—a weapon that was particularly useful at close range and aboard ships, which often became fields of battle after being boarded by hostile forces.

The question of the sword being a primary or secondary weapon is one that often overlooks the martial artist's training and outlook towards warfare. Although he may have had his preferred weapons such as the Roman soldier did, this did not hinder him from employing other weapons when the need arose. To be unable to do so would result in a dead warrior, and no matter how brave the warrior, no matter who he was, most if not all relished the thought of living to see another tomorrow.

Secondary Systems. If there was any one system that was used in conjunction—though secondary to the sword—it would be empty-handed forms of fighting. The pre-modern martial artist was skilled in almost all facets of combat, empty-handed techniques were not unknown to him and most were practiced in kata or pre-arranged methods of training. However, they were not considered a primary means of conducting combat; instead they were used only as a last resort, or an instance in which grappling came about and the enemy had to be thrown or held for the warrior to make better use of his dagger or sword. This is not to say that these methods of empty-handed combat were ineffective, but the early martial artist's realm of combat was dominated

ROMAN "MAINZ" STYLE GLADIUS (RIGHT), ROMAN "POMPEII" STYLE GLADIUS(LEFT), BOTH STYLES OF THE GLADIUS COULD BE USED FOE EITHER CUTTING OR THRUSTING.

by the use of weapons and armor; therefore, he relied upon his weapons first. To hit an armored foe with your empty hand, no matter how well-trained the fighter may be, will not have the effect that a sword or glaive's cut will. Dr. Yang Jwing-Ming wrote about the Chinese and their use of weapons,

> Generally speaking, a well-trained martial artist would carry at least three kinds of weapons. He would have a primary weapon such as a sword, saber, staff, or spear, with which he was most proficient. A secondary weapon would be hidden on his body, per-haps a whip or iron chain in his belt or a pair of dag-gers in his boots, which could be used in the event that his main weapon was lost during battle. For use at very long distances or in a surprise attack in a close battle, he would use dart weapons.
> —(Yang, *Ancient Chinese Weapons,* 5)

For the Japanese, *Jujutsu* was used in conjunction with the samurai's main weapons—the sword, spear, and naginata. Grappling could and did occur on the battlefield, therefore, the various locks and holds found in classical *Jujutsu* were used as a means to twist, turn, throw, or bend an opponent into a position from which the samurai could better use his weapon. The term

"Submission Fighting" had an entirely different meaning to the samurai and other men-of-arms, because for them the submission hold was merely a means to keep their opponent in place while they killed them with a well-placed stab of the dagger or cut from a sword. Even the use of striking, although not unknown, could and did prove to be ineffective on the battlefield due to the use of body armor.

For European martial artists, wrestling was stressed not only for its combative aspects but also for developing stamina and strength, both of which were needed on the battlefield. Throws, counter-throws, locks, strangulation methods, kicks, and hand strikes were all included in the training. Despite the fact that such methods existed and were widely known, they were still used in a manner secondary to those weapons used by the man-of-arms. As it was with the Japanese, unarmed opponents on the field of battle would have stood little or no chance against a mounted knight or armored pike-man no matter how skilled they might have been with their feet and fist.

Cut or Thrust. The techniques of cut, thrust, and guard have remained primary in the art of fencing since the birth of the sword. Sir Richard Burton wrote about the process of the sword's evolution and its use that, "The sword has three main uses, cutting, thrusting, and guarding. If these qualifications could be combined, there would be no difficulty in determining the single best shape. But unfortunately—perhaps I should say fortunately—each requisite interferes to a great extent with the other. Hence the various modifications adopted by different peoples, and hence the successive steps of progress." (Burton, *Book of the Sword*, 128) The cut and thrust have influenced the practice, training, kata, and design of swords for thousands of years. In fact, fencing systems have been built around each one of these techniques in both Western and Eastern societies with mid-nineteenth century European military fencing is one such example. By 1845 A.D. it was divided into three distinct systems. First, was the small-sword used extensively in duels and relied heavily on thrusting techniques; the second was the curved blade saber system that was based upon cutting techniques; and the third was a

GREEK KOPIS

combination cut and thrust system that relied upon straight bladed weapons. However, it is due to the preference of sword, metal used to make it, historical period of its use, cultural mores, and even geographical region, that the emphasis placed upon cut, thrust, and guard has varied, and has resulted in a vast amount of sword styles and many different methods of training.

The use of cut or thrust has spurred heated debates for thousands of years as to which is the better method of attack. Sir Richard Burton wrote in 1883 A.D. that, "Indeed, the man who first 'gave point' made a discovery which more than doubled the capability of his sword." (Ibid., 127) Some eighty years later Ewart Oakeshott wrote, "but a man's instinct in a fight is to slash at his foe, for his natural blow sweeps round in the segment of a circle centered in his shoulder. To strike out straight is an acquired art, easily forgotten in the heat of battle." (Oakeshott, *The Archaeology of Weapons,* 26) Although both men's observations are valid, the impetus for using either the thrust or cut is one that is often heavily influenced by the type of combat engaged. For instance, the man-of-arms who fights with a sword on horseback may prefer a cutting action, which often results in the use of a curved blade sword. This is because as he charges past his opponent the momentum of the horse, combined with the blade's curve, will give increased power to his cut. The blade's

THE ESTOC. ITS BLADE HAD NO CUTTING EDGE AND COULD ONLY BE USED FOR THRUSTING.

shape will also allow the rider to cut through his opponent without stopping. However, if a thrust was performed using a straight blade, the sword could become embedded in the enemy and this would leave the rider without a weapon, due to the fact that his horse's momentum had driven the sword's blade so far into the opponent's body that it could not be easily extracted. For the warrior who fought on foot against an armored foe, a thrust performed with a straighter and thinner blade that would penetrate armor was more effective because the momentum found in the cavalry charge was not present: thus, the swordsman had a better chance to use a thrusting action. Conditions like this resulted in the development of swords such as the *estoc*, which was popular during the Middle Ages of Europe and used specifically by warriors to thrust in openings found in an opponent's armor. Using the *estoc*, and those pre-arranged training routines inherent to its practice, made liberal use of thrusting actions. The weapon's birth also gave rise to its techniques and pre-arranged forms.

Cutting, thrusting and the combination of the two, which is a cut and thrust blade, have all been employed on the battlefield throughout history. In some instances the blade—although designed primarily for cutting such as the Japanese *katana*—could also be used for thrusting. While in others, the sword was designed for one specific purpose, as was the Abyssinian *shotel*, whose long curved blade was used to reach behind the shield of an enemy. Such differences are indicative of a culture's martial ethos and the conditions under which it waged war.

To many European swordsmen, the *shotel's* appearance was ugly. Some considered it an eyesore, a weapon not even worth picking up. Richard Burton wrote about the *shotel* and its curved blade that,

> Nothing less handy than this gigantic sickle; the edge is inside, the grip is too small, and the difficulty of drawing the blade from the scabbard is considerable. The handle, four inches long, is a rude lump of black wood, and the tang is carried to the pommel and there clinched. The coarse and ugly blade has a mid-rib running the whole length, forming a double slope to the edges; it is one inch broad at the base, and tapers to a point that can hardly be used. The length along the arc is three feet thirty-seven inches; the curve, measuring from arc to chord, is two inches; and the projection beyond the directing line is four inches. The rough scabbard of untanned hide is shod with a hollow brass knob, a ferule ruder even than the blade; and a large iron buckle affixed to the top of the scabbard under the haft, connects with a belt or waist strap. Such a weapon never belonged to a race of Swordsmen.
>
> —(Burton, *The Book of the Sword,* 163)

It is easy to see how Burton, who was a very skilled swordsman trained in the European schools of fence, would hold such views towards a weapon like the *shotel.* The weapon is not appealing to the eye, and the skill and finesse often found in those methods with which Burton was familiar were not present with the *shotel.* The purpose behind the weapon's development was different from that of the *epee* or saber. Its blade was curved to attack a foe that held a shield in front; for that, the *shotel,* no matter how unappealing it may have looked, was well suited.

The preference for the thrust or cut and the weapons so closely associated with them are also based on cultural and nationalistic traditions. This resulted in training pattern kata being developed within and becoming to specific cultures and societies. The training patterns used with the *shotel* were native to the region in which the sword was developed. They were influenced by the local culture and its ways of warfare. The weapon itself was a reflection of these forces and in fact, became a cross current for the Abyssinian culture and its martial traditions. Burton's views and opinions about swordsmanship were influenced by his own social and cosmological experiences, which differed from those of the Abyssinian. Yet it was these experiences that often influenced the practice of a fighting art and its kata. For Burton, the lunge executed with an *epee* and the saber's cutting stroke were both commonplace techniques during his sword training. This is because of his culture's traditions that dictated how the sword should be used—traditions that did not include the prospect of reaching behind an opponent's shield with a curved sickle. Such an idea would have probably been considered outside the realm of true swordsmanship for many of Burton's fellow citizens, especially for those whose practice was done exclusively within the confines of the nineteenth century fencing hall. However, for the Abyssinian who used the *shotel* on tribal battlefields and to whom Saint Augustine's "Just War" doctrine was not known, nor any of the traditions associated with the Western martial arts, the idea of using the curved sickle to strike an enemy who used a shield for protection, was perfectly acceptable. He placed no value on the duel as Burton knew it; his weapon was designed for a specific purpose and its use required an entirely different sequence of movements than what Burton used in his fencing. The Abyssinian would crouch low to the ground, bob, weave, and hop from position to position trying to gain an advantage over his foe. He did not intend to stand erect as was done in the fencing halls of Europe, and this was reflected in his technique. When these two cultures with their different martial traditions met on the battlefield, those who were the best trained and had the most effective martial art, would be on the side that prevailed; yet even for the victor, the experience would often lead to a reassessment of their techniques and tactics, as well as the pre-arranged methods of training used.

SHOTEL. ALTHOUGH VERY UNGAINLY IN APPEARANCE THE WEAPON IS NONE THE LESS VERY WELL SUITED FOR THE TASK THAT IT WAS DESIGNED FOR. WITH THE WEAPON'S DESIGN ALSO CAME A SYSTEMATIC METHOD FOR ITS USE.

Due to the pragmatic environment of the battlefield and the various weapons used during combat, the issue of whether to cut or thrust for the warrior was a relatively simple one; he had to be able to perform both actions. His preference for either action may have been reflected in the weapons he carried, such as his sword being more suited for cutting, but he would also have a weapon that had the ability to thrust. If this could not be done with his sword then it would be with another weapon in the form of a spear, dagger, short sword, etc. Likewise, his array of weapons would enable him to cover all distances of combat, be it long, medium, or short range, and often when he fought in all three ranges during the course of a battle. His spear or *naginata* would cover long range, the sword or axe would be used at mid-range, and at close range he would employ a short sword, dirk or dagger. The following illustration explains the ranges and some of the weapons used in combat at those ranges.

Interestingly enough when one examines the methods of battlefield combat conducted between 1400 B.C. and 1500 A.D., there are many similarities in the tactics and weapons as well as the transmission and practice of techniques. Ewart Oakeshott reflected upon this when he spoke about the 3,000 year tradition of sword and shield. Likewise, Alfred Hutton made the same

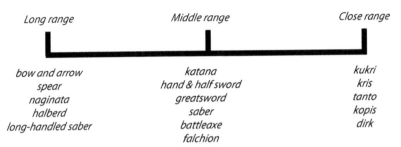

Long range	Middle range	Close range
bow and arrow	katana	kukri
spear	hand & half sword	kris
naginata	greatsword	tanto
halberd	saber	kopis
long-handled saber	battleaxe	dirk
	falchion	

observation when he stated, "When we come to examine the various systems of hand-to hand fighting, there is no need to go back to the remote ages of nations dead and gone; the Assyrians, the Greeks, and the Romans all wore armor, and all fought with spears and swords and shields, differing more or less in fashion and in form, but in their use varying scarcely at all from the weapons of the armor-clad knights of the Middle Ages" (Hutton, *The Sword and the Centuries,* xiii) Despite the culture and time, the objective of battlefield combat remained the same within most societies. Armies clad in armor met on the battlefield with spear, sword and shield. They then proceeded to try to kill one another as the engagement was first conducted at long range through use of bow and pole-arm, and then progressed to middle range with use of sword or axe, and then for a few unlucky souls, on to close range were deadly struggles with dagger and empty hands occurred. This pattern remained the same for close to 3,000 years in both Western and Eastern cultures.

Eduard Wagner remarked about pre-modern martial arts that, "Cut and thrust weapons belong to the category of cold weapons which, in hand-to-hand fighting, are wielded exclusively by the strength of the human arm. That is why they were not subject to such swift and substantial changes as firearms, which only began to be used at the end of the fourteenth century, and yet by the first quarter of the fifteenth were already acquiring great significance on the various fields of battle." (Wagner, *Cut and Thrust Weapons,* 21) This is very true whether the martial art was of Eastern or Western heritage; the driving force behind its techniques was manpower and muscle. However, there were, variations in the execution of combat, even when the use of cut and thrust weapons was at its prime. Hutton wrote of this when he penned, *The Small Sword is the Call of Honor, the Back Sword the Call of Duty.* (Hutton, *The Sword and the Centuries,* 286) Weapons and their respective systems are different; the backsword was intended for use on the battlefield where hacking and chopping actions were used often during melee combat. The thrust was used, but the warrior, more than likely, fought as he could, having no time to square off with an opponent; his terms of engagement often placed more emphasis on inflicting a mortal wound. Due to his realm of combat being filled with many armed opponents, therefore, the sequence of blocking or parrying with his sword, then following up with a riposte was abandoned in favor of covering with his shield and then counter attacking, or avoiding the enemy's attack and then countering.

Hutton's writing placed the small sword and its thrust squarely into the civilian's realm of fighting, a method absent of the battlefield, where body armor was not to be found. The division Hutton made between civilian weapons and those used on the field of battle is also found within systems related to civilian and military fighting arts, as well as the kata used within them. Just as Burton's statement reflected upon the differences found between his worldview and that of the Abyssinian warrior who used the *shotel,* there also was a division to be found between the civil and military fighting arts and the way they were conducted. Although there were murderous intentions associated with each system, the environments and methods associated with both forms of fighting differed. These differences greatly affected the goal of each system's techniques and how they were practiced.

3-2 CIVILIAN FIGHTING ARTS

As we examined earlier, the term 'martial art' is used today in a very generic manner to describe any and all forms of fighting, particularly those of Asian traditions. This is not an altogether accurate use of the term; in fact it can be a very misleading one. Depending upon the time and culture, pre-modern civilian and military systems would differ not only in the environments that they were used, but also in their techniques, tactics, weapons, and pre-arranged training sequences. The early *Okinawan te* practitioner might have spent hours perfecting his straight punch on a *mikawara* board. His knuckles needed toughening to ensure a better punch, and from his practice he not only achieved this goal, but he also developed a bio-mechanical response that was very crucial for the proper execution of his technique in the high stress atmosphere of combat. He trained himself to fight an opponent who recognized the same rules of engagement as he did, rules under which the use of empty-handed techniques was perfectly acceptable and on par with the society's customs, where unarmed fighting in the civil sectors was commonplace. In comparison to the Okinawan, the Japanese samurai would have perfected his sword skills. This is because unlike the Okinawan, he was in possession of a weapon, and the likelihood of the samurai engaging in an unarmed brawl, as the Okinawan would, was highly unlikely. If such an instance did arise, the samurai would merely have drawn his sword and cut down the would-be attacker. It was a distinct possibility that the Japanese martial artist would meet an armed foe, either in daily life or on the battlefield, therefore his fighting art was based on the use of weapons.

In his recollections of a lifetime spent studying karate, famed Okinawan Master Shoshin Nagamine wrote of his experiences of training with Motobu Choki, whose philosophy about the kata of Okinawan karate was as Nagamine recalled, "In his later years Motobu told me that the applications of kata have their limits and one must come to understand this. The techniques of kata were never developed to be used against a professional fighter, in an arena, or on a battlefield. They were, however, most effective against someone who had no idea of the strategy being used to counter their aggressive behavior." (Nagamine, *Okinawa's Masters,* 96) Likewise, Donn Draeger, in writing about the differences between civil and military systems stated that, "Many of the commonman's systems are basically unarmed methods for dealing with an adversary, for the good reason that his socially superior overlords proscribed the bearing of weapons to all but the elite, hereditarily legitimized, professional warrior class. Thus it was that in contradistinction to the aristocratic warriors and

their martial arts, plebeian man developed civil arts of defense."
(Draeger, *Martial Civil Dichotomy*, 7) Both statements provide
much insight into the civil fighting arts and the development of
their kata. This kind of system's intended purpose was usually
not for the battlefield, but as protection for daily life during
which the civil practitioner did at times encounter trained men
bent on harming him. In such cases, the civilian had no choice
but to stand and fight. When this occurred, the civil practitioners often found themselves at a disadvantage because their
weapons and systems of fighting were developed for self-protec-
tion, instead of battlefield combat.

At various times, and within certain cultures, the distinction
between civil and military fighting arts is not so clear as is found
between the Okinawan and Japanese fighting arts. For the
Englishman of the sixteenth century, the two methods often
went hand-in-hand and martial/civil fighting arts were practiced
by a majority of the culture's populace. Terry Brown wrote of the
English martial arts that,

> It is clear from these sources that martial arts have
> always been held dear by Englishmen, which is not
> surprising when one considers how frequently during
> its early history England was raided and invaded.
> With these facts in mind the passion of the English
> for martial arts can be seen as a zeal for their freedom
> and independence, though, like modern martial
> artists, they were also concerned for their personal
> safety because, in times past, England suffered levels
> of social violence that make modern society seem, by
> comparison, like Utopia."
> —(Brown, *English Martial Arts*, 14)

Many Englishmen of this time, both of the aristocratic and
common class, carried weapons. It was in fact the commoner's possession of arms that allowed him to have social and democratic
rights, since the British government was afraid of armed rebellion.
Since the populace as a whole was trained in the use of arms, when
the army's ranks needed to be filled for battle, it was the monarchs
who turned to the British people. Although the fighting arts prac-

ticed may have been used extensively in civilian realms, it was only a small step for them to be employed on the battlefield.

By the fifteenth century A.D., systematic teachings and schools of both civil and military fighting arts could be found throughout Eastern and Western societies. Due to thousands of years of combat conducted both on and off the battlefield, the art of hand-to-hand fighting evolved into a sophisticated science. Uniform methods of teaching were developed to pass on this pugilistic knowledge, many were taught by established organizations and schools. In some cultures, these had existed for hundreds of years, while in others their foundation was a new endeavor, based on techniques that had withstood their trial by fire. For the Chinese, boxing, wrestling, and weapon arts have been an integral part of their country's long and illustrious history. One of the first known references to systematic methods of teaching Chinese fighting arts was found during the Han dynasty of 206 B.C. to 220 A.D. It was then that the *Six Chapters of Hand Fighting* were discussed in the *Han Book of Arts* or *Han Shu I Wen Chih*. (Draeger, Smith, *Comprehensive Asian Fighting Arts,* 16) In Japan, systematic methods of teaching or *ryu-ha* came into being during the Heian period of 794-1185 A.D. and would remain the mainstay of transmission until modern times. In England, Henry the VIII gave royal sanction to the establishment of the "Masters of the Noble Science of Defense" and forbade anyone who was not a member of this organization to teach martial arts in England. Richard Cohen wrote about the organization's establishment,

> Well aware that young men versed in swordsmanship would be a valuable asset in wartime, Henry VIII invited the best-known teachers in the country to join a new, royally sanctioned academy. On July 20, 1540 A.D. he granted a license to certain "Masters of the Noble Science of Defense," simultaneously outlawing independent practitioners. He forbade anyone who was not a member of his new institution from teaching and obliged all members to swear not to instruct murderers, thieves, or other undesirables.
>
> —(Cohen, *By The Sword,* 31)

In central Europe, two of the best known and prominent schools of arms were the Marxbruder and Federfechter guilds, which were formed by craftsmen such as potters, carpenters, shoemakers, goldsmiths, etc. These were not the only cultures to develop systematic teachings and organized schools. The Filipinos, Koreans, Burmese, Spanish, French, Indonesians and many others also did the same.

In examining the civilian fighting arts and their methods of pre-arranged training, there are three basic areas that they can be divided into. They are:

1. Weapons
   Staff and stick
   Bladed
   Agricultural
2. Empty-handed methods, including striking, grappling, kicking, joint locking.
3. Combative sports

Each of the above is a major component of the civilian fighting arts their practice and pre-arranged training routines have all been distinctly affected by the civil environment. As it was with the man-of-arms who had to make his weapons and systems of fighting conform to the environment of the battlefield, so too was it with the civilian fighter whose weapons, systems of fighting, and kata had to meet the demands of his field of combat. For the civilian, his opponent may not have been clad in armor from head to foot wielding a halberd or battleaxe, but nonetheless a rapier's thrust to the chest or dagger's slash to the throat would prove just as lethal as a cavalryman's spear thrust. Since he wore no armor for protection, the civilian had to rely extensively on parrying, blocking, footwork, and evasive body movements to avoid being seriously wounded or even killed. Likewise, since he was not on the battlefield but conducting business in daily life, his weapons had to conform to the society's social settings and acceptable norms of behavior. While an eight-foot spear or two-handed great sword may have been commonplace on the battlefield, for the carpenter, shoemaker, or craftsman walking through crowded streets during his daily affairs such weapons would have been out of place and very uncomfortable to carry about. However, to carry a dagger, small sword, cane, or walking stick would have been perfectly acceptable and easily done. The restrictions placed by governing authorities on the use of weapons by a populace greatly affected the manner in which civil fighting arts and their pre-arranged forms developed. For the seventeenth century Okinawan, owner-ship of a sword was strictly forbidden by the occupying Japanese; therefore his study and practice of the fighting arts revolved around empty handed methods and the use of everyday imple-ments such as the *kama*, staff, etc. In sixteenth century England, Queen Elizabeth ordered that no rapiers be over a yard in length, and those that were longer were to be broken off at a yard. This was done not only to curb violence, but also in an attempt to cur-tail the growing length of swords at the time. Elizabeth's actions affected swordsmen of the day because the shortened rapiers translated into quicker movements performed at closer range, so different tactics and techniques had to be adopted during the practice of fighting arts.

From such circumstances as these, civil forms of fighting came to have distinct characteristics that differed from those of the military. For instance, a *taijiquan* sword forms' techniques may appear light and agile in execution by comparison to those of a *naginata* kata. The *taijiquan* form (or kata) was built around techniques that were intended to be used against an opponent who wore no armor, as opposed to the classical *naginata* kata. These variances in both kata and technique were not limited to just those bladed weapons used by the civilian practitioner, but to all realms of his fighting arts, especially those un-armed meth-ods that relied heavily upon the use of throws, kicks, punches and other methods of empty-handed striking.

Civil Weapons. Although the civilian may have preferred a hand and a half sword, spear, halberd or even a *katana*, if he did not have the money to purchase such a weapon, and if laws were in place that prevented him from carrying arms, then he had to make due with other objects to protect himself and his family.

Such circumstances have resulted in a wide variety of weapons and training patterns.

Staff and Stick. Of all the weapons used in the civil fighting arts, the one found within most systems regardless of culture, location or time, is the stick, be it the staff, cudgel, or baton. Perhaps this is because the weapon itself is simple to make and easy to obtain. From early Egypt to modern times, it is a weapon that has proven to be one of the most reliable that man has ever known; the staff, cudgel or short stick, doesn't misfire; if made of sturdy wood hardly ever breaks; it can be used in almost any condition such as extreme cold or heat, rain, sleet or snow; and will last a lifetime. It has often been used as a training device in place of bladed weapons, that would allow sparring and even employment of bladed techniques in a non-lethal manner. During the nineteenth century, cane fencing became very popular in Europe; the cane was both a practical and safe weapon, one that was carried by many gentlemen in daily life. Christoph Amberger wrote about its use and role in society during this period that, "Singlestick (German: Stockfechten or French: canne) was popular throughout the nineteenth century, when no gentleman would have been caught dead on the street without his walking stick. Cane fencing and singlestick became synonymous toward the end of the nineteenth century, and many military manuals treat canes as training weapons for the saber and broadsword." (Amberger, *Hammerterz Forum,* Winter 1995/96) The movement patterns and strikes associated with the staff, cane, and even the small stick are very similar to those found in many sword systems. In fact, the trajectories traveled by these weapons when they are used to strike, are often exactly the same as those traveled by a sword performing a cutting stroke.

Dave Lowery wrote about the similarities found between the short staff, *katana*, spear, and *bo* that, "The *jo* possesses many of the attributes of all three of these revered arms: the slashing stroke of the *katana*, the thrusting reach of the spear, and the reversible striking power and indestructibility of the *bo*. It is little surprise that, for all its simplicity, once its development began, a forest of schools and masters soon sprang up to further refine and perfect the *jo* as a formidable weapon." (Lowery, *Classical Japanese Martial Arts*, 21) The short staff or cane however, unlike its bladed counterpart, could be grasped along any portion of its length and this in itself made the weapon extremely versatile in that it could be employed in a wide variety of ways. Furthermore, the cane or short staff is a very unassuming weapon that can easily be carried in day-to-day life. That in itself was often a deciding factor in the weapon's employment.

In terms of national identity, the art of stick and staff fighting has many homes; however, its place within the folds of Irish culture is legendary. To carry the short staff or *Bata* as it is known in Gaelic, was considered a mark of honor that symbolized the transition from boyhood to manhood. It was a rite of passage the Irish took very seriously. The various strikes, parries, and pre-arranged patterns associated with the *bata* were passed on from father to son, generation after generation. Sparring played a major role during training and it was not uncommon to see young men engaged for lengthy periods in free fighting, perfecting their thrusts, parries and strikes. Much like the Okinawans with their native karate systems, the *bata* was associated nationally with the Irish, but within the Irish culture different styles of using the bata were found due to geographical, political and family preferences.

The Irish were not the only noted short staff fighters of the European fighting arts. The seventeenth century Carniolans were noted for their cudgel skills. Carniola, which was part of the Holy Roman Empire and located in Austria, was divided into five regions: upper, lower, middle, inner, and Istria. Each region had a specific type of cudgel and style of fighting associated with it. For instance, the upper Carniolans preferred a heavy knotted stick that was thick at its top portions and thin at the bottom. These short staffs were very lethal weapons and their users could kill with a single blow. The lower Carniolans preferred thinner, more agile walking-type canes, which although not as heavy as their relatives in upper Carniola were still effective as weapons. The Istrians carried a staff with a crescent blade attached to its end. The weapon doubled as a staff, but also a weapon with which they could cut their foe. For the English, the cudgel and singlestick were used similar to the Scottish broadsword, yet with less of a chance of being killed during prize fighting. Often the participants in these events would stand within limbs' distance of one another with their left arm tied into position and their right arm free to use their weapon. They would then begin to engage in their bout with the intention of inflicting enough pain to make their opponent relinquish the match. Alfred Hutton wrote about the practice, "The object of these encounters was to break the opponent's head—that is to say, so to strike it as to draw a stream of blood an inch in length; and no hit on any other part of the person was recognized at all." (Hutton, *The Sword and the Centuries*, 348) Despite the fact that these bouts, were conducted as prizefights, the techniques used were nonetheless very effective and quite applicable for use with an everyday walking cane during the course of one's daily life. As the sword came to be worn less often due to social mores and laws which prevented the wearing of weapons in public, the cane became a prominent fixture of men in society. In fact, its popularity grew to a point in nineteenth century Europe where several different styles and schools of cane fencing flourished.

For Asian practitioners the short staff was also a popular weapon and came to be used within many different systems. In both the internal and external forms of Chinese fighting arts the long and short staffs are used, with some versions of the short staff made from iron and referred to as a whip rod. It was not uncommon to find hand protectors on these weapons. The staff, both long and short, reflects the movements of the system that employs it, such as in *taijiquan* where sliding, coiling, sticking, four corners repelling and neutralizing, and other concepts of movement used within the empty hand forms are also found in staff training. For the Japanese the *jo* first became incorporated into the *Koryu bujutsu* during the Muromachi era. Although initially partial to the six foot *bo*, the *jo* became favored due to its size and efficiency—the very same reasons that made the weapon so popular in the European fighting arts. As Dave Lowry wrote about the short staff and its popularity within the Japanese martial arts, "Martial scholars estimate that nearly 350 other classical *Bugei-ryu* subsequently adopted various *jo* techniques in their schools. The methods of classical *jojutsu* contained within the kata of these *ryu* are incredibly diverse, dealing with every possible situation in which the practitioner might find himself." (Lowry, *Jo: Art of Japanese Short Staff Press*, 25) The cane and short staff's popularity was widespread throughout many societies' fighting arts; in most instances, its practice was done with almost every possible intention in mind. However, its popularity as a weapon did not outshine other staff weapons, for both the *bo* and quarterstaff

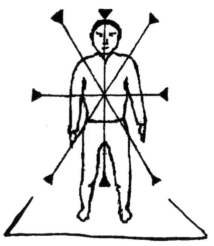

THE EIGHT BASIC TRAJECTORIES OF ATTACK WITH THE CANE, CUDGEL, OR SHORT STAFF. THESE TRAJECTORIES ARE ALSO FOLLOWED IN BOTH EUROPEAN AND ASIAN COMBATIVE ARTS AND CAN BE USED FOR EITHER CUTTING OR THRUSTING WEAPONS SUCH AS THE KATANA, BROADSWORD, KUKRI, RAPIER, ETC.

enjoyed much use in many different systems of fighting.

Bladed Weapons. The bladed weapons employed by the civilian fighter run a wide gambit of styles and systems, many of which could be used to both cut and thrust. The weapons themselves can be categorized into two basic realms: long and short blades. Long blades are those such as the rapier, small sword, *epee*, Filipino *kampilan*, (a weapon whose blade was often coated with poison before combat), and the Chinese scholar's sword. These are weapons whose length permitted a stand off distance between two opponents of three feet or more. In discussing the differences between the Chinese martial sword and the scholar's sword Dr. Yang Jwing-Ming wrote, "In fact, because the martial sword is much heavier than the scholar sword, the martial sword can also be used as a battle weapon. However since the scholar sword is light and its killing potential relatively weaker than the martial sword, the scholar sword is commonly used as a defensive weapon only." (Yang, *Ancient Chinese Weapons,* 61) His observation holds true for other blades used widely by civilian fighters that were not nearly as lethal as their military counterparts because of their size and that they were not designed for use against an armor clad opponent. Likewise, geographical, religious and cultural preferences dictated a weapon's shape and the corresponding training patterns used with it. Fighting arts with Islamic, influences such as those found in Indonesia and the southern Philippines favor cutting weapons, often with curved or semi-curved blades. This is possibly because the origins of Islam are found in a nomadic culture that placed much emphasis on mobile warfare, and raiding in particular. Thomas Arnold wrote of the Ottomans and their cavalry that, "The weapons of choice remained the light lance, the scimitar and, above all the bow." (Arnold, *Renaissance at War,* 120) These traits of Islamic warfare carried over into other cultures and influenced their fighting arts as Islam spread. Moro tribesmen of the Philippines would etch on the blades of their Barongs: "There is no God but Allah." (Wiley, *Filipino Fighting Arts,* 120) As these influences moved from horse and camel-based cultures to those that were not, so to did the preferences in weaponry. In terms of geographical influences we once more will refer to Dr. Yang, who wrote about the northern and southern schools of Chinese sword that, "Generally speaking, the length of the sword used by southern martial artists was shorter than that of the northern martial artists. This is because the southern martial artists specialized in short-range fighting techniques. Long swords would not be practical for these techniques." (Yang, *Ancient Chinese Weapons,* 62) This was also seen in other cultures; for instance, the Gurkha's *kukri* is a short-bladed weapon very well suited for chopping. Used within Nepal as both a weapon and agricultural tool, the preferred method of use for the *kukri* on the battlefield was to infiltrate an enemy's position and get close enough to where there was no choice but to fight hand-to-hand. In such cases the enemy usually stood little or no chance against the Gurkha's slashing strokes. In contrast to the Gurkha, the eighteenth century Frenchman preferred to use the small sword, which was designed specifically as a thrusting weapon.

NINETEENTH CENTURY SINGLESTICK FENCER: THE USE OF THE CANE, SINGLESTICK, AND SHORT STAFF REQUIRED FINESSE, TIMING AND MUCH PRACTICE. COMPETITIONS FOR THE SINGLESTICK BECAME WIDELY POPULAR AT COUNTY FAIRS WHERE STAGES WERE BUILT AND CONTESTANTS FOUGHT TO THE SPECTATORS' DELIGHT.

Lightweight and easy to wear, it was an extremely deadly instrument with a triangular shaped blade that could easily penetrate a man's clothes, passing into his body where a fatal puncture wound would be inflicted. Countless hours were spent in search of the perfect thrust, practicing the parries, passes, and counters that made up the small sword's array of techniques.

In many instances the wearing of a long bladed weapon both on and off the battlefield, has been associated with a society's elite. In Japan, to wear the twin swords, or *dashio*, was a right assigned to only those of a samurai lineage. Even when he was not on the battlefield, the swordsman's skills were adapted to the civilian world where armor was not worn. This adaptation spawned new methods of fighting and new kata, for like the European gentleman who traveled with his small sword or rapier, the samurai in his day to day life was also presented with the possibility of engaging an un-armored foe. While this may have given him more body targets to strike, he too was without armor.

It was from such circumstances that *iai-jutsu* evolved. Although the samurai traversed the battlefield with his sword already drawn, it was in urban areas where the need to defend himself against ambush required him to quickly use his *katana.* Therefore, he came to the realization that the quicker he could draw his sword the faster he could use it, and if he could both draw and strike with his weapon then his chance for survival

IAI-GOSHI

would be greatly increased. It is the initial draw and cut with the sword that is the basis for *iai-jutsu,* with any subsequent cuts thereafter being considered *ken-jutsu. Iai-jutsu* made use of a quick cutting or thrusting action in conjunction with the sword's draw, and accuracy was of extreme importance. The optimum desired effect was to draw, cut and kill, all in one quick motion. The samurai studied

human anatomy extensively, finding the most vulnerable areas where he would direct his attack, thereby allowing him to cut down his opponent in the most effective manner. Unlike *ken-jutsu,* whose katas were primarily performed in two person sets, the *iai-jutsu* kata were practiced solo. Drawing, then cutting from both standing and sitting postures was performed repeatedly. The samurai would stand or sit in during the course of his day; they were not fixed fighting stances, as are often seen displayed in modern tournament forms, but instead natural relaxed postures. The samurai had to be able to draw and cut without any forewarning; therefore *iai-jutsu* draws were executed from common postures preferably which were *iai-goshi,* a semi-seated position, and *tachi-ai,* a standing position. These two positions allowed him the most mobility and greatest range of movement with his sword.

Iai-jutsu, unlike its battlefield counterpart *ken-jutsu,* is primarily a defensive method used in response to an attacker's actions, although this does not necessarily mean that the samurai always waited for his opponent to attack him. Given the threat presented, it was often the person whose sword was drawn first that lived, while the other died with his blade still in its scabbard. *Iai-jutsu* was divided into four compartments—the draw, the cut, the removal of blood from the sword, and returning the sword to its scabbard. All of which were performed by the skilled swordsman in a composite manner. (Draeger, *Classical Bujutsu*, 70) To do otherwise, or any deviation from the prearranged sequence, would have been considered poor form and very dangerous since *iai-jutsu* was practiced with a live blade.

The clothes a person wore had much to do with how a fighting art was practiced. In times past, the more elegant the clothes worn the more money the individual had and often enjoyed a higher status within society. It was not uncommon for the tastes of nobility to dictate the type of weapon used and the way combat was waged within a society. At times this was based not so much on a particular system's effectiveness, but instead upon the ruling class' preferences. In Elizabethan England such tastes are why the Italian Rapier became popular among the uppercrust of English society, and with it came imported hilts, which were handsomely decorated and adorned, as well as other items of Italian manufacture that British society valued. Vincentio Saviolo and other Italian swordsmen attained social grace and recognition, not so much for their skill of arms, but for the appeal of their gentlemanly ways, grace at dance, and the fact that they belonged to affluent Italian families. Saviolo's social standing was very much in contrast to the English masters-of-arms, who did not belong to the upper class, but rather were

TACHI-AI

craftsmen, butchers, candle-makers, and people mostly of the common class who did not, or could not, grace society's courts. The Italians cast a shaded eye upon the English masters-of-arms despite the fact that the English were as skilled, if not more so, than they were.

Before long, Saviolo opened a school of fencing in London, much to the dismay of the London masters of defense, who held disdain for not only his style of fighting, but also because he was taking money from their pockets. Saviolo's style of fighting, unlike that of the English, was more suited for the duel, not the battlefield or rough and tumble world of English street brawling where the broadsword and quarterstaff were used extensively. The Italians tended to specialize in the use of the rapier, while the English made use of sword, quarterstaff, dagger and unarmed methods of fighting. Theirs was the fighting art of the soldier and not the courtly gentlemen. One Englishman who sought to avenge the Italian incursion, a Austen Bagger, went to Rocco Bonnetti's house armed with sword and buckler and challenged him to a duel. The Italian, who was enraged at the challenge, rushed from his house with a two-handed sword to deal with the rude individual but his only accomplishment was to be badly beaten and humiliated. Saviolo himself was dealt such treatment when he abruptly and rudely, refused an offer to visit an Englishman's school. The English master-of-arms struck the Italian about the head and ears with his fists, knocked him to the ground, and then poured a glass of ale over him, a response very different indeed to the ones he was accustomed to. Later Saviolo survived a duel by simply refusing to fight it. He had been challenged by English master George Silver, whose treatise on the art of fighting, *Paradoxes of Defense,* was widely read at the time. Saviolo ignored the offer, which although caused him to lose face, earned him the title of a "Better Christian than fighter" from George Silver.

The Italian schools succeeded because of political clout and ties with English nobility, and in fact became partially responsible for the demise of the traditional English martial arts. The English systems had long been considered part of the common-man's survival. As Puritanical sentiments grew in the country that eventually placed restrictions upon many forms of public entertainment, prize-fighting being one of them, the centuries-old traditions of the English martial arts faded, only to be replaced by those of the Italian schools, which although held more appeal were much less effective methods of fighting. In turn, the art of fencing became the sport of nobility and not the common man's fighting art as it once had been.

Short Blades and Truncheons. The use of short-bladed weapons and truncheons by the civilian fighter run the gambit from the standard dagger or dirk with its double-edged straight blade that could be easily concealed in ones clothing, to the exotic Deer Hook Sword of *Baguazhang* and the *karambit* used within the Indonesian fighting arts. The *karambit* itself is a weapon that fully embodies the realm of civil fighting arts, because it is meant to be used against an opponent who preferably is not armed. Under such circumstances, it proves itself very effective especially if used to cut upward into one's bowels, inner thighs, or arms where major arteries lay close to the skin. The *karambit* is a fierce looking weapon that is easily concealed, and can inflict great damage on a foe. However, with its short length and design that allows little blocking or parrying if used against an opponent armed with a long blade, staff, or cane, the *karambit* practitioner may find himself at a disadvantage.

cutting edge

"Karambit." The weapon is not much bigger than a man's hand and can be held with the forefinger inserted through the ring and blade extended, or retracted. There are many variations to this weapon but all maintain the basic claw blade design that is good for ripping and puncturing. It is a weapon best used at close range against an unarmed foe. Its use is limited in battlefield combat.

The Deer Hook Sword or Deer Antler Saber is named so because of its design that looks much the same as a pair of deer antlers. It can be used for chopping, cutting, thrusting, hooking, or parrying and is an all-round versatile weapon save for the fact that it requires use at close range. The weapon itself is used in *Baguazhang* training and is incorporated into the empty-handed movement patterns found within the system and its forms. The weapon emulates *Bagua* in that it is employed in slipping, sliding, rotating, spinning and turning motions, all of which are characteristic of the *Bagua* system. (Yang, Liang, Wu, *Baguazhang*, 293)

The correlation between the Deer Hook Sword and the empty-handed techniques and movement patterns of *Baguazhang* can also be found within other civil fighting arts and their pre-arranged training routines. Okinawan systems frequently interchange weapons such as the *sai*, *tonfa*, *kama* and even the *bo* with the empty handed katas of the various *ryu*. Likewise the practice of the traditional *kobudo* katas in an empty-handed manner is also encouraged. This practice can be seen in the performance of *sai* katas such as *Kusanku* and *Kusanku-Sai* and has been done with other items such as hair pins. This interchanging of weapons with empty-handed kata can and does have a multidimensional effect, for not only does it make the civil fighting arts exponent proficient with a weapon, but it also serves to incorporated the weapons techniques and tactics into the empty-handed realm of fighting. This can result in new areas of interest such as more focus being placed on the attacking of limbs through the use of strikes, or actions being practiced due to the inclusion of weapons that previously had not existed. The influence of weapons upon civil fighting arts is not limited to just pre-modern methods but has also affected those in contemporary times. In examining the influence that Western fencing had on *jeet kune do* Richard Cohen wrote that,

> Lee produced a seven-volume work entitled The Tao [Dao] of Jeet Kune Do. In it he reproduced long extracts from the writings of Julio M. Castello, C.-L. De Beaumont, and especially the French Master Roger Crosnier. He also borrowed extensively from works on boxing, kinetics, and philosophy, throughout replacing the words 'fencer' with 'fighter,' 'blade' with 'arm,' and 'fencing' with JKD (jeet kune do). The rationale of this mishmash is that, as masters often refer to one's chosen weapon as an extension of ones fencing arm, why not close the distance and use one's arm as if it were a sword?
>
> —(Cohen, *By the Sword*, 133)

Though Lee's system contemporary, the process Cohen describes has happened in earlier times; the jab found throughout Western methods of boxing and unarmed combat was greatly influenced by the fencers lunge. It should also be kept in mind that this garnering of techniques from one system to another works both ways. While in Okinawan Karate the empty-handed methods incorporated armed methods into the pre-existing kata, in other cultures, such as the Filipino and Burmese fighting arts, empty-handed methods of training evolved out of armed methods of fighting. For the Bando player, the execution of empty handed *Kukri* techniques is highly encouraged and can in fact yield a completely new method of fighting.

The truncheon is its own weapons system, and yet is also interchangeable with bladed and empty-handed methods of fighting. Although it has many styles and is used throughout the fighting arts, the weapon's use remains primarily a short weapon with blunt edges that can be used to either block or strike. Perhaps the most famous of all truncheon weapons is the *sai*, or short sword of karate, as it is commonly called—although it is not a sword by any means. The weapon's evolution in the Chinese fighting arts is believed to have started as a hairpin,

THE SAI IS JUST ONE EXAMPLE OF THE TRUNCHEON BEING USED WITHIN THE CIVIL FIGHTING ARTS. ALTHOUGH USED THROUGHOUT THE ASIAN FIGHTING ARTS ITS DESIGN REMAINS PRIMARILY THE SAME. ALTERATIONS ARE NOT UNCOMMON THOUGH, SOMETIMES ONE TINE WILL BE TURNED UPWARDS WHILE ONE IS TURNED DOWNWARDS. OTHER VERSIONS INCLUDE THOSE WITH ONLY ONE TINE. THE MARK OF A GOOD SAI PRACTITIONER IS THE EASE WITH WHICH HE CAN EXTEND AND RETRACT THE WEAPONS BLADE AWAY FROM HIS FOREARM DURING PRACTICE.

many of which were used as weapons, and then slowly over time became the *sai*. For the Chinese, as with other fighters, the *sai* is considered a close range weapon, that can be used to strike, stab, or even entangle an opponent's weapon with its twines. It was a weapon favored by the Taiwanese and in Canton and Fujian provinces.

Within the Indonesian fighting arts the *sai* is known as the *tjabang* by *pentjak-silat* practitioners and the *titjio* by *kuntao* experts. Its use in the Indonesian fighting arts predates that of the Okinawan and Chinese methods, and the weapon was quite possibly exported to both of these cultures from Indonesia. For Okinawan fighters the *sai* is legendary within the culture's fighting arts and is found within all of its karate *ryu-ha*. Many of the island's leading *karate-ka*, both of contemporary and pre-modern times, have been noted for their *sai* skills. The weapon can also be used as a projectile. This technique is found throughout Okinawan *sai* kata, either simulated or performed by throwing the *sai* point first at the ground in an attempt to impale the opponent's foot, even pinning it to the ground, and likely a third *sai* is drawn from the practitioners obi and the kata continued. Overall, it is an extremely versatile weapon, that requires little upkeep but still proves to be very effective in the hands of skilled practitioner.

"CROSS BUTTOCK" ALTHOUGH BOXING IS CONDUCTED WITH ONLY THE FISTS TODAY, IN THE MID NINETEENTH CENTURY IT WAS A STYLE OF FIGHTING SUITED FOR BOTH THE RING AND STREET. IN ENGLAND DURING THE LATE EIGHTEENTH CENTURY, THROWS, CHOPS AND HAMMERFISTS WERE ALL LEGAL. FIGHTING WAS ALSO CONDUCTED WITH BARE KNUCKLES. BY THE TURN OF THE TWENTIETH CENTURY BARE KNUCKLE FIGHTING WAS CONSIDERED UNLAWFUL IN ENGLAND AND CONDUCTED ONLY BY AMATEURS.

Empty Hands. During the practice of a fighting art, it is not uncommon for exponents to conduct their studies with such a microcosmic viewpoint that they develop a limited horizon, focused only upon a particular system or style. Although distinctions can be made between systems based upon geographical, cultural, historical, and even religious reasons, there still are similarities to be found within all systems, particularly those that deal with empty-handed combat. In examining the differences between Eastern and Western methods of empty-handed fighting, one of the most distinct is the use of animal forms within Asian systems of fighting and their absence in Western methods.

The use of pre-arranged sequences named after specific animals that embody the traits of the animal in technique, or body movement, is a method found within almost all Asian empty-handed fighting arts. In Asia, man studied animals and how they fought, then used their strategies and movements to his own advantage. However, just because it is a widespread practice does not mean that it is overly regimented, since the characteristics of each animal form will vary between styles and sub-systems and even between individual practitioners. Phillip B. Zarrilli wrote about the use of animal forms in *kalarippayattu*,

> The specific form of any pose, as well as its qualitative dimensions are open to interpretation. The specifics of what is or is not considered correct differ widely from master to master and style to style. Even among masters who had the same teacher and are from the same linage of practice, differences are common. Each master believes that his own interpretation, practice and style, are the correct way of performing a form or the correct method of application.
> —(Zarrilli, *When the Body Becomes All Eyes*, 93)

Zarrilli's words can also be applied to other systems as well. The karate kata *Chinto* is practiced in a great many of the Okinawan *ryu-ha's*; however, its appearance differs from *ryu* to *ryu*. Likewise, in Burmese Bando, a tiger slap in one system may be referred to as an eagle or leopard slap in another. The boar system is noted for its rushing, crushing, and charging tactics, all of which seem to be of an external nature, yet the boar system embraces hard, middle, and soft elements within its array of teachings.

The utilization of animals as mediums to express the art of fighting within the Asian methods is a result of geography and culture. In terms of geography, the animals and reptiles often referred to in the Eastern systems are, in many instances, only found within specific geographical regions located in the Asian continent. The tiger did not reside in Western Europe, nor did the cobra or the leopard; therefore, their use as methodologies to define the Western fighting arts are almost non-existent.

However, certain animals were not unknown in Western mythologies; Adam and Eve were betrayed by the serpent, dragons and lions populate ancient Western folklore, as do other animals, some of which are real while others are not. The Greek myth of Theseus killing the Minotaur or bull of Minos is one such example. The Minotaur was in fact a mythical representation of the leading commander of Minos' military and it was he who Theseus defeated and not a half-bull, half-man creature. Yet a good deal of the animals that are used as mediums of expression in the Asian fighting arts are also to be found in Western Europe, the boar, eagle, bear, and deer are all animals native to the region. Thus, the reason for their use in Eastern fighting arts as opposed to those in the West is based on cultural mores aside from those imposed by geographical boundaries.

The monastic tradition found within Asian religions is also found in Western societies. Within Eastern religions it evolved into an institution from the Indian tradition of the roaming monk who lived on the edge of society, with each Buddhist monk tracing his linage back to the Buddha. For Christian traditions it is believed that the monastic practice began somewhere around the third century A.D. when St. Anthony began establishing communities for those who wished to live and study together. Yet the two religions took different views to the world around them.

For the Christians, although nature was appreciated, God was the omnipresent force that controlled and gave birth to all things. Though he gave birth to all things he was still considered separate from his creations; they were a part of him. As Karen Armstrong wrote about mans earliest perceptions of God, "Unlike the pagan deities, Yahweh was not in any of the forces of nature but a realm apart. He is experienced in the scarcely perceptible timbre of a tiny breeze in the paradox of a voiced silence." (Armstrong, *A History of God,* 27) Being that he was the God of man, all other forms of life were considered subservient to mankind and the separation that existed between God and nature also came to exist between Western man and the world in which he lived.

In Buddhist tradition, the view is held that the world is there to remind man of all things living. To be released from his suffering, man has to live a life that shows compassion for all living things; the totality of life itself cannot be summed up in mere words but only felt and experienced. Joseph Campbell wrote that,

> Similarly, throughout the Orient, throughout the ancient world, and in pre-Columbian Americas, society and nature represented to the mind the inexpressible. "The plants, rocks, fire, water, are all alive. They watch us and protect us," declared an old Apache storyteller, "and it is then that they reveal themselves and speak to us." This is what the Buddhists call "the sermon of the inanimate."
> —(Campbell, *The Hero with a Thousand Faces*, 169)

These variances in worldviews are also found within each culture's fighting arts and are increased more so by the philosophical views of each society.

The West had such philosophers as Aristotle, and with the Greek's discovery of formed logic in the fourth century B.C., it gave man the power of deductive reasoning—to be able to set and analyze a problem and eliminate any ideas not pertaining directly to the matter itself. While this was a giant step forward in the Western world, it also had a negative impact in that it put forth the idea that a few simple deductions could unlock the mysteries of almost anything. This led to a very pragmatic view towards combat, both civil and military. In Western methods, it also isolated the act of fighting from the same mediums of expression that were incorporated into Asian systems. Unlike his Shaolin counterpart, who defined his fighting style through the use of the tiger, crane, or deer, the hoplite did not look upon his actions in the same way. The phalanx was not viewed as a herd of storming tigers, but instead as a unit of warriors trained and equipped to do battle. In contrast the Shaolin, Buddhist, or Daoist monk viewed his world through the elements and animals that surrounded him. Although both he and the hoplite had their gods and deities, the Shaolin monk used these very same forces to define and study his fighting arts. In fact he was encouraged to do so by his religious and philosophical views.

With the decline of the monastic system in Europe, Western man's separation with nature increased. Robert Thurman wrote about the decline of the tradition in Europe and its impact,

> The actual person, along with God, got abstracted out of existence, subtracted from what matters. The corresponding northern European destruction of monasticism as a balancing force in society resulted in a 'this-worldly asceticism,' wherein the entire life energy is turned over to worldly activity, which is self-less in that it lacks ultimate fruition. It was natural that material progress became a new absolute, infinite in horizon, with the removal of the medieval notions of life in balance with nature and of nature as sacred in the sense of being God-created. By the seventeenth century, these trends had developed a full head of steam. The cosmos was seen as a mechanism, perhaps started by a divine artificer and scientist but now running on automatic."
> —(Thurman, *Inner Revolution*, 243)

Thus, instead of using natural forms or animals as mediums to define the fighting arts, Western societies came to rely upon logic, science, mathematics, and a very pragmatic philosophy that distanced the Western practitioner from the world in which he lived, but yet, at the same time gave him the ability to kill with almost complete impunity. William Manchester stated about Western societies and the martial-religious bond within them, "Soldiers of Christ swung their swords freely. And the victims were not always pagans. Every flourishing religion has been intermittently watered by the blood of its own faithful, but none has seen more spectacular internecine butchery than Christianity." (Manchester, *A Word Lit Only by Fire*, 7) Although religious, scientific, and philosophical ideas were instrumental in the Western traditions for either condemning or justifying the act of war, they would not serve as animal-based methodologies through which either military or civil forms of fighting would be viewed or based.

In Asian cultures, war was also waged on the grounds of religious or philosophical ideals. The Asian man-of-arms, just as his

Western counterpart, could kill with a sense of impunity and indifference towards an enemy, and he often did. S.R. Turnbull wrote of how Zen Buddhism appealed so strongly to the samurai, "How, then, could a mystical religion of contemplation appeal so strongly to the samurai, when they were men of action? The answer lies partly in what Zen offered, for it provided essentially a way of salvation which the believer worked out for himself, and this would find great sympathy among the wielders of bow and sword." (*The Samurai, A Military History,* 85) Yet within this religious based justification for killing, there was also a strong appreciation for the world in which the samurai lived. It inspired them to interpret their world through that which surrounded them; to quote D.T. Suzuki who wrote about the relationship between Zen and nature, "A man of *fuga,* therefore, finds his good friends in flowers and birds, in rocks and waters, in rains and the moon." (Suzuki, *Zen and Japanese Culture,* 258) It was this way of thought and its embracement of nature, which was found in Buddhism, Daoism, and Shinto practices, that helped influence the use of animals as a mediums to interpret the fighting arts. For those systems affected by western philosophies they are expressed in what seems to be a very cold and calculated manner, whereas many of those influenced by eastern religion and philosophy use the tiger, deer, cobra and other animals as mediums to interpret and explore the art of fighting.

Despite the philosophical differences in expression of Eastern and Western fighting arts there are many similarities to be found between the two. In his examination of Okinawan karate's styles and teachers, Mark Bishop quoted *Kushin-ryu* chief instructor Shintaro Yoshizato as saying, "the katas are all very much alike, after all a man has only two hands and two feet, and his movements are very limited." (Bishop, *Okinawan Karate,* 105) His statement applies to not only Okinawan methods but also those of both Eastern and Western fighting arts. It is from the construction of the human body that only so many movement patterns can be executed; therefore, commonalities will exist. A Cross-Buttock Throw in English wrestling may be known as "Squeezing the Neck, Hip Throw" in Chinese wrestling, or in

Judo it appears as a variation of *koshi guruma,* also known as the hip wheel throw. This is also true for punching techniques, the same fist techniques of Burmese Bando can also be found in Okinawan karate, and Chinese and Western styles of boxing. It is not uncommon to find the same strike used in both Asian and European fighting arts. Consider the straight punch and the uppercut. Both are used extensively in western boxing as well as within a wide range of Asian civil fighting arts like karate, Shaolin kung fu, Thai boxing, *taijiquan* and *Baguazhang.* Furthermore, early Western boxing was also noted for its use of chops, hammer-smashes, slaps, and gouges. To say that discourse between two cultures brought forth similarities in their fighting arts is a fair and valid assumption, however, similar needs in the realm of empty-handed fighting contributed greatly to the development of these techniques and probably did more for their evolution than discourse between Western and Eastern societies.

The majority of people are born with two arms, legs, hands, feet, ears and eyes; obvious reasons that our body imposes upon our execution of technique encompassing years of evolutionary behavior. The chopping, and thrusting actions that man first learned at early stages of his development are the very same that gave birth to the sword's cut and thrust. These are also the foundations upon which many empty-handed methods of fighting and their kata are based. The thrust of the arm forward or upward is also the foundation for the jab and straight punch, while the chop forms the basis of the *shuto*, slap, and even back-fist. Below are some examples of the techniques used in the fighting arts that are based upon these two principles of arm and hand movement.

Thrust	**Chop**
Straight punch	Tiger Claw
Twist Punch	Hammer Smash
Jab	Ridge Hand Strike
Heel Palm Strike	Hook Punch
Cobra Strike (Bando)	Monkey Slap
Viper Strike (Bando)	Fair Lady Plays Guitar
Right and Left Cross (Boxing)	

Along with some other animals on the earth, man is born totally defenseless, he has no claws, armor or fangs. He cannot run as fast as the gazelle, deer or even a small rabbit. Therefore, we can safely say that due to this handicap, mankind started near the bottom of the food chain. Necessity is the mother of all invention, and this position in life made early man acutely aware of the need to defend himself. This in itself is one reason why the urge to employ weapons in combat is so strong within the human race. It was a trait developed early in our history, one that has become almost instinctive. Prehistoric man's predators were much larger and stronger than he was, therefore some means had to be developed to even the score, and raise his chances of survival. Rocks, bones, and sticks served first, followed by more sophisticated weaponry. Before there were weapons, prehistoric man had to make due with his hands and feet for self-defense; from this experience the foundation for empty-handed fighting was laid. It was with the chop or thrust of the hand and stomp of the foot that he lashed out at that which hunted him.

Perhaps one of the most instinctive reactions of empty-handed combat performed the world over is to grapple, or more precisely strangle one's enemy. It is, pure and simple, a survival skill that takes no training and can be a very simple, yet effective technique, especially in the heat of battle. While using his limbs to strangle, hit, and stomp man also learned to fend off blows by covering with his arms, hence the ability to block. Of the five skills used in all forms of empty-handed fighting—striking with the hands, kicking, grappling, blocking, and joint locking—four of them have been in existence since the beginning of mankind. The foundation for empty-handed fighting and the multitude of systems related to it were formulated even before man had developed the means to speak, read, or write. More often than not, inspiration for his earliest empty-handed techniques was devised in the heat of battle. They were not formulated or manufactured first then used later, as many of his weapons were. Instead, his divine inspiration and method of discovery came when the lion or tiger attacked or when he lashed out at another as he fought over food.

MUHAMMAD ALI EXECUTING UPPERCUT

Combative Sport. The recorded history of empty handed fighting dates back many thousands of years. Early Egyptian hieroglyphics show fighters boxing and stick fighting both of which the Pharaohs encouraged. Chinese wrestling methods of Shuai Jiao were practiced and perfected in 2697 B.C. by both civilian and military practitioners and by the Song Dynasty (960-1278 A.D) had become very complex in its execution and techniques. Japanese sumo wrestling's history can be traced back to 23 B.C. when Nomi-no-Sukune bested Tajima-no-Kehaya by breaking his ribs with a well placed kick. (Draeger, *Asian Fighting Arts,* 131) In examining the empty-handed fighting arts there is a strong bond found between them and combative sports. Shoshin Nagamine wrote on the Okinawan form of wrestling *tegumi,* "It is believed that grappling ascended from primitive man's instinctive means of self-preservation. In the history of civil fighting traditions here in Okinawa we refer to such grappling concepts as *tegumi.* There is every reason to believe that *tegumi,* after being enhanced by techniques of striking and kicking, also served as the progenitor of *te.*" (*Nagaminie, Okinawa's Master,* 138) Okinawa is not the only culture in which its civil fighting arts have been heavily influenced or evolved out of combative sports: however, the term 'combative sports' our contemporary methods, or when compared to those of pre-modern times ours are very tame. William Manchester discussed the medieval world and the levels of violence found within it,

> The levels of everyday violence—deaths in alehouse brawls, during bouts with staves, or even in playing football or wrestling—was shocking. Tournaments were very different from the romantic descriptions in Malory, Scott, and Conan Doyle. They were vicious sham battles by large bands of armed knights, ostensibly gatherings for enjoyment and exercise but really occasions for abduction and mayhem. As late as 1240, in a tourney near Düsseldorf, sixty knights were hacked to death.
> —(Manchester, *A Word Lit Only by Fire,* 6)

Early combative sports such as sumo wrestling, *vajra-musti*, Thai boxing, *pankration*, Greco-wrestling and others like them embraced the ethos of their day and age. They were bloody and brutal affairs, what we today would consider a back alley brawl or even murder instead of a sporting contest. Many of these early "sports" were also used on the battlefield to capture one's enemy or for defense in case the warrior found himself unarmed. For instance, early sumo techniques included both hand and foot strikes. *Pankration* strikes were used against all parts of a contestant's body, eyes and genitals included; it was a very lethal fighting art either in or out of the arena. These methods and others like them were considered sports only because the normal method of conducting battlefield combat was with weapons and in armor. Apart from that, most were very effective methods of unarmed combat that would heavily influence later methods of civil fighting.

In time, as battlefield methods became more complex and their weapons came to be the property of the ruling class, the empty-handed forms of civil fighting became divided from battlefield and sports systems. In terms of battle use, the matter was simple; the empty hand does not possess the killing power of the sword, bow, or spear therefore, systems based on its use came to be used extensively in the civilians word where body armor was not worn and the outbreak of a fistfight was not uncommon. If such systems were used on the battlefield, they were done as a last resort. This even proved true in many early societies in which the civilian carrying arms was not all that uncommon. The Englishman who held a quarterstaff in his hand was sure to use it, before he would use his bare knuckles. Likewise, the Filipino who worked the sugarcane and rice fields would rely on his *bolo* for defense more than his hands and feet.

However, the division of civil empty-handed methods from the sport realm was due to several factors, such as the introduction of weaponry into the civil fighting arts—an act that also influenced how empty-handed fighting was conducted—the adaptation of military training methods, philosophical ideologies such as Daoism and Muslim religious beliefs being incorporated,

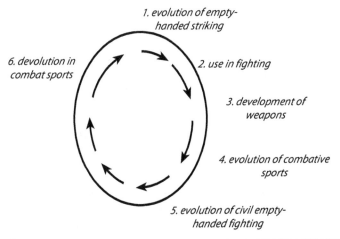

1. evolution of empty-handed striking

2. use in fighting

3. development of weapons

4. evolution of combative sports

5. evolution of civil empty-handed fighting

6. devolution in combat sports

ILLUSTRATION OF THE EVOLUTION OF EMPTY-HANDED FORMS OF FIGHTING FROM EARLY MAN, TO THEIR DEVOLUTION INTO MODERN-DAY COMBATIVE SPORTS. THERE ARE EXCEPTIONS, IN SOME CASES CIVIL FIGHTING CAME FROM PRE-EXISTING WEAPONS SYSTEMS.

as well as a host of other cultural, geographical and social factors that all helped give the civil fighting arts a distinct flavor. Still, the influence of combat sports was felt, since challenges and tournaments frequent almost all forms of civil fighting, and both employ similar methods of kicking, striking, and grappling. Perhaps one of the best examples of the civil fighting art-combative sport relationship is the playing of the prize by English fighters during the sixteenth and seventeenth centuries. To advance through the ranks of the English schools of fighting, public challenges were held in which the fighters were placed on stage and then conducted their bouts. This ensured that they passed their examination before a public forum and that their skill levels were exhibited for all to see. During these matches contestants fought with broad sword, quarterstaff, sword and buckler, and empty handed. Such contests drew large crowds and were considered to be hardy entertainment. However, as time passed and social mores changed, the use of weapons came to be abandoned and boxing took their place. Despite the similarities between civil empty-handed methods and combative sports, on the field of battle both were considered secondary systems because it was here that the sword's edged blade, the arrow's flight, and the spear's point ruled supreme.

Fear and the Ties that Bind. One underlining trait of almost all pre-modern systems, whether for the battlefield, sport or use in civil fighting, was the utilization of sound and effective techniques. This process began in the earliest periods of history, where the basis for all fighting arts was to fight, either on the battlefield, or as with prehistoric man, to protect himself from predators. As man began to study and store techniques and tactics, two types of movements were recognized, that formed the foundation of all his techniques—those that were executed in a natural manner and those which he learned. The International Hoplology Society classifies human movement patterns into two categories. They are "primary movement patterns" and "secondary movement patterns." Primary movement patterns are those that we do naturally and increase in their complexity as we develop and mature from infant to adult. A child grabs hold of its bottle, which is a primary movement, but by the time it has reached adulthood, the grab can be applied to numerous things and in under a great many circumstances. Secondary movement patterns are those that have to be learned such as walking, climbing, jumping etc. Both of these types of movement patterns are found within kata, either civil or military, and are used in unison. An example of the two movements being used together would be the Greek hoplite and the phalanx formation. Those who made up the phalanx wore heavy armor and were armed with six- to eight-foot spears. Due to the close confines of the formation the hoplite could only use his spear in one of two manners either as an overhand thrust, which is a primary movement pattern, or an underhand thrust, which is a secondary movement pattern. These techniques were performed within the phalanx and had to be learned by the hoplite. On a more individual level, an open-handed slap would be considered a primary movement pattern and can be used quite effectively in a combative scenario. In contrast to the slap a straight snap kick would be considered a secondary movement pattern and has to be taught to the fighter for it to be used.

In each case, be it civilian or warrior, more often than not the number of techniques retained was slight, and each was perfected by the warrior to a high degree. As Mr. Armstrong said about the role of kata and pre-arranged movement patterns, "The purpose of kata (or any pre-arranged movement pattern (PMP) designed for combative application) was not to develop the individual's ability to respond to any attack with the choice of a wide variety of techniques, but to train that individual to effectively utilize a select few proven techniques in response to a wide variety of attacks or combative situations." (Armstrong, *Hoplos,* Winter 1988 Vol. VI, No. 1&2)

In hand-to-hand combat, especially with edged weapons, fear often proves to be as great an enemy as your opponent. This is because fear induces paralysis, reduces motor functions, and often makes even the most conditioned responses become difficult to execute. Italian fencing great Aldo Nadi testified firsthand to the effects that fear has on one engaged in mortal combat. In 1924 he was insulted by Adolfo Contronei, who was the fencing editor of the *Corriere della Sera,* a Milan newspaper. Nadi, seeking to defend his honor, issued a challenge to Contronei who accepted. The two men met at the San Siro racetrack in Milan. Although Nadi was a championship fencer whose skill was legendary, he had never fought a duel before. In contrast to the young champion was Contronei, who, although a much older man, had fought and survived five previous duels. On the agreed day Nadi arrived at the racetrack to see Contronei chatting nonchalantly with his seconds. As Nadi prepared for the duel, the referee fastened a white silk handkerchief to his wrist. Inquiring what it was for, the young champion was told that it was to protect the main arteries in his arm. Nadi later wrote about his duel and described in part his feeling and techniques during the action.

> You counterattack, and your sword-point lands precisely where you wanted it to—at the wrist, piercing both the glove and the white silk. However, during your opponent's flurry of action his blade clashed with yours, and its point whips into your forearm…
> "Halt!" shouts the referee. Oblivious to your own wound, you look at once at your opponent's wrist, then up at his face. Why on earth does he look so

> pleased? Wasn't he the one to be hit first? Yes, but this
> is not like a competition bout. He has every reason to
> be pleased at having wounded you...
> —(Cohen, *By the Sword*, 290)

Although both men survived the duel, Nadi's performance was less than spectacular. In competition his form was picture perfect; however, during the duel, it was much more like that of a novice fencer instead of the champion he was. Pictures taken during the duel show Nadi's left foot far off the ground during the lunge, his left arm well out of position, leading foot misplaced, and other mistakes commonly associated with beginning fencers.

Nadi's paralysis is precisely why the movements found within pre-modern and even today's combative forms are of a pragmatic and simplistic nature. They were designed and practiced to ensure a quick resolution to the engagement. The closer the movement was to its actual application the easier it was to execute during the heat of combat. Movements done for aesthetic appeal had no place in the realm of combative kata. Pre-modern training routines and kata were built from techniques the warrior had used successfully. They were in turn practiced by people who had first hand combat experience, or by those uninitiated to the battlefield but with full understanding of their combative applications. These were violent times and kata mirrored that violence, yet their usefulness would come to exceed those of just the combative realm.

CHAPTER 4

Kata, Metaphors, and Nuances

The battlefield is symbolic of the field of life, where
every creature lives on the death of another.
                                        —Joseph Campbell

Warfare is one of the most complex experiences that man
endures, for within its realm there is violence, bloodshed,
courage, honor, fear, and terror, as well as happiness and rejoic-
ing. The act of fighting is in itself a mass of contradictions all of
which make up the sum total of the fighting arts. However, to
explore and understand this complex experience and all of its
contradictions, it is necessary to bring some form to its chaos to
separate the substance of fighting from its matter, for without
substance there is only chaos and no way to understand or interpret the experience itself. In his long standing work, *The History
of Western Philosophy* Bertrand Russell, while examining
Aristotle's *Metaphysics*, made the observation about established
forms and their relationship to mankind, that by creating form
man is not giving birth to something new, for the elements of his
creation already exist; he instead is merely giving substance and
shape to an experience where there was none. To quote Mr.
Russell, "The form of a thing, we are told, is its essence and pri-

mary substance. Forms are substantial, although universals are not. When a man makes a brazen sphere, both the matter and the form already existed and all that he does is to bring them together; the man does not make the form, any more than he makes the brass. Not everything has matter there are eternal things, and these have no matter, except those of them that are movable in space. Things increase in actuality by acquiring form; matter without form is only potentiality." (Russell, *The History of Western Philosophy,* 166) While man does not create form because its elements are already present, he can give form where there is none and in doing so, bring together those elements that are of both a physical and non-physical nature. This he does with kata.

To give form means much more than arranging physical objects in a symmetrical pattern. Instead, to give form to something is to bring together elements of a physical and non-physical nature. For example, when artists create paintings, they do so with more than just brush strokes. The painting is a physical expression of creativity; it comprises many years spent training, the artist's emotions, intellect, ideas, and ethics. When the painting is put on display and viewed by others, this wide range of physical and non-physical elements is brought together as a single entity, that is the painting itself.

This process of bringing form to man's world is done through other mediums as well, such as poetry. The poem is an intersection of man's creativity with the world in which he lives. The poem is a reflection of both his world and his views of the world, a reflection with an almost bottomless depth to it.

Likewise, the same holds true for the practice of kata. Man did not create kata per se, for its elements already existed. He instead gave form to the chaos of combat by bringing its various elements of both physical and non-physical nature together. In giving form to combat, he incorporated not only codified techniques, but also the warrior's emotions, ethos, and worldviews. By doing so his kata increased in its actuality and potentiality, and just like poetry, art, and literature, kata came to embrace much more than just physically-based techniques. Kata, like poetry became a reflection of the world in which he lived.

With Mr. Russell's statement in mind, it should come as no surprise that the fighting arts' kata and pre-arranged training sequences became metaphors for man to express other realms of his existence. Since a high degree of discipline is needed in the practice of a martial art, courage to perform combat and a strong inner awareness to face death on the battlefield, the warrior ethos came to represent much more than just warfare. It stood for courage, hard work, dedication, creativity, and spiritual development. In 1 Cor. 9: 25-27 Paul, uses the fighter as metaphor in explaining how self sacrifice and discipline was needed to attain a spiritual harmony and a closer relationship with God when he wrote:

> 25 And every man who battles in the contest
> frees his mind from every
> Thing else. And yet they run to win a garland,
> which is perishable; but we
> To win one which is everlasting.
> 26 I therefore so run, not for something that is
> uncertain; and I so fight,
> Not as one who beats the air.
> 27 But I conquer and subdue my body so that,
> by no chance, when I have preached to oth-
> ers, will I despise myself.
> —(1 Cor. 9:25-27)

Paul trains not so much to win a contest but instead to conquer himself. Although Paul's training is of an entirely spiritual nature, he still uses the fighter as a metaphor to explain the rigors and dedication involved in his spiritual quest. Likewise, the Greeks understood the benefits gained from practicing combative sports, as character development was of prime interest to them. The complete man was both scholar and warrior in their society; therefore, in addition to sports serving as a medium through which the Greeks expressed their philosophical, physical, competitive, and ethical views—all within the rings' confines—the games of Greece were also a unifying factor of their society. All warfare was stopped in observance of the Olympiad so that the populace could witness the physical feats and heroics of the contestants, particularly those of the fighters. William Durant wrote about the Olympic Games in Greek society that, "Religion failed to unify Greece, but athletics—periodically— succeeded. Men went to Olympia, Delphi, Corinth, and Nemea not so much to honor the gods—for these could be honored any- where—as to witness the heroic contests of chosen athletes, and the ecumenical assemblage of varied Greeks. Alexander, who could see Greece from without, considered Olympia the capital of the Greek world." (Durant, *The Life of Greece,* 211) These were endeavors through which the fighters' actions imparted moral lessons. In doing so the Greeks combative sports came to serve as examples of the character development process that could be attained through severe training. Just as karate-do, *tai- jiquan, iai-do,* and other modern systems are valued for their inner-development process, so too it was that with the ancient combative sports of classical Greece, became metaphors for the traits most valued in the Ancient Greek society. It came to be understood that everything did not rest upon the event itself but in the process of training for the event. The punching of the bag, constant practice of techniques, shadow boxing, physical condi- tioning, and the ever present self-analysis that fighters use to cri- tique both their technique and mindset, were just as important if not more so to the fighters over-all development, as was the win- ning of the event.

In reflecting on his over forty years' training in the Chinese fighting arts, Dr. Yang Jwing-Ming wrote about the transforma- tion process involved with his own training,

> I remember that my White Crane master told me something that affected my perspective of Chinese martial arts completely. He told me that the goal of a martial artist's learning was not fighting. It is neither for showing off nor for proving you are capable of conquering other people. He said the final goal of learning is to discover the meaning of life. Therefore, what I was learning from him was not a martial art, but the way of life. I could not accept this concept when I was young. However, now I am more than fifty. I can start to understand what he meant at the time."
>
> —(Yang, *Taijiquan, Classical Yang Style,* 25)

Dr. Yang's statement reflects much on the process of personal development associated with martial arts practice, and one of the major vehicles to explore the human experience is kata. Kata and pre-arranged training routines pits the fighter against himself and forces him to come to terms with both his physical and spiritual limitations. By practicing the form, the student comes to see its almost endless realms. Just as the constant recital of poetry can bring forth new understandings of the poem, so too the study of kata can become an alternative to combat, the moral, philosophical, and symbolic meanings of which often become lessons with more to do with one's conduct and life, or conduct *in* life than combat itself.

In modern times, one reason for this alternative form of practice is due to the widespread use of firearms that has made many of the hand-to-hand based systems obsolete. In other instances, it is because a society's religious and philosophical doctrines have become intertwined with a fighting art, and in doing so have brought about a depth of study based on metaphysical realms as well as those of a physical nature. For instance, in *taijiquan* it is believed that through constant practice one can achieve enlightenment. However, to do so requires the practitioner to be able to control their *Qi* or *Chi*, and to be able to move this inner force in prescribed patterns that circulate throughout the brain, abdomen, spleen, lungs, and even blood cells. A large part of learning how to move *Qi* is through the constant practice of the *taijiquan* forms—the same ones that also teach combative techniques. This dual emphasis of practice has been present in *taijiquan* for hundreds of years and has gone hand in hand with the systems practice throughout most of its existence. Thus, what can be deemed a higher art evolves from the practice of forms.

The birth of the fighting arts' kata was initiated when man's creativity intersected with his need to preserve and transmit battle proven techniques. In doing so he also incorporated both spiritual and physical elements into his forms to further aid him in dealing with the brutal world of hand-to-hand combat. However, as time passed from the initial point of the kata's con-

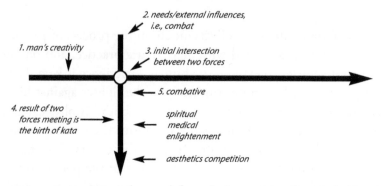

ception, its practice changed from being primarily combative in nature, embracing other elements such as enlightenment, medical and/or health issues.

The above illustration shows the evolution of forms practice. Man's creativity (1) intersects with a need for some method of retaining and transmitting techniques (2). These forces come together (3), which results in the conception of kata (4). In the bottom right area (5), we can see how the initial purpose of kata was based on strictly combative needs, but as time passes and the kata grows distant from its original point of conception, the reason behind its practice change as is seen in number 5. This change of outlook towards kata practice can be seen in many systems, some of which have been in existence for hundreds of years. However, the change can also be viewed as the kata being studied with a somewhat higher aim in mind, rather than just combat. The practitioner comes to understand that the kata's foundation rests upon combative laurels then in turn begins to seek out a higher level of personal awareness through kata practice. This results in the kata serving as a metaphor for one's own inner development, a so-called awakening to the innermost parts of the human being. It also results in the practitioner becoming educated in the various levels of development found within kata practice where what appears to be superficial at first glance is in actuality a very complex endeavor.

In *The Statesman,* Plato uses art as a metaphor to illustrate how there are various levels of perception, performance, and execution to be found not only in politics, but also in many other endeavors that are associated with life. Some of these levels of perception are obvious, while some are not. Plato illustrates this when he uses the conversation between the stranger and a young Socrates as an example:

> Stranger: There is such a thing as learning the princi-
> ples of music or the principles of any of the crafts, is
> there not?
> Young Socrates: Yes
> Stranger: But are we willing to admit that there exists
> an art of a higher order also concerned with this
> process of acquiring special skills? This second art is
> the one whose province is to decide whether or not
> we ought to learn any particular art.
> Young Socrates: Yes, we will attest the existence of an
> art of this higher order.
> Stranger: We must also agree then, that it is to be dis-
> tinguished from all arts of the lower order.
> Young Socrates: Yes

The art of a higher order that the Stranger speaks of is not separate from art but is found within art. For example, there are novice wood workers and master wood workers. To the inexperienced eye there is no difference between the two as they go about their work. However, in viewing the work of each one, the difference in skill levels will be quite noticeable. Whereas the novice woodworker's finished piece will look rough and unpolished, the master's will have finesse to it. The novice's work will go against the grain and shape of the wood, but the master's will flow with it. The novice's techniques will look sophisticated and difficult while the master's will appear simple and easy to execute. During the process of creating the artwork there also will be a difference between the two craftsmen; the novice will view his work in a one-dimensional manner, for he is merely carving or turning a piece of wood. However, for the master woodworker the creative process involved will have an entirely different meaning. From the long years of experience upon which he draws, less often means more; less force in his knife strokes, less wood cut away. For the master the process of creating a piece of art goes beyond the mere physical realm of cutting, sanding and carving. It is a means through which the master woodworker can both express and explore his creativity and at times his own spirituality. It is this unseen inner level of awareness that separates the master woodworker from the novice. For the novice, the piece of wood is everything; however, for the master, it often is secondary to the creative experience itself and all that it entails.

The piece of work can also suggest another realm of meaning. A wood-turner 200 years ago made a wooden bowl for utilitarian reasons. He needed something from which to eat, so he carved a simple bowl. Time passed and the need for the wooden bowl as a kitchen implement decreased. Yet, should the simple wooden bowl survive for 200 years without being broken, it becomes a valuable artifact that is a link to an era long past. Even though this wooden bowl is no longer in use, it is considered important because of its age and historical significance. It appeals to a new generation of people, perhaps from an aesthetic or historical perspective. Kata, just like the wooden bowl, will hold different meanings for different generations of people. Just as a society's values and outlooks change with time, so to will the role of kata. What was once valued for its combative application, in turn comes to be appreciated for its esoteric realms; or perhaps the physical dexterity required in its performance will be valued strictly for health benefits instead of its usefulness on the battlefield. Thus, the kata that may have not changed physically comes to be valued differently from how it was originally conceived.

Kata of Karate. One of the more popular fighting arts today is Okinawan karate. From Okinawa, the art of karate has spread worldwide and has given birth to many subsects and offshoot styles, some of which are very traditional in their approach such as the Japanese *Wado-ryu*, while others are a hybrid blend of both old and new. For today's karate-ka to have knowledge of ten, fifteen, or even twenty different kata is not uncommon. Often within a year, the beginning karate-ka will be able to execute as many as five different kata, some of which will encompass 50 movements or more. This approach to practicing kata is done more for the sake of preservation, for just as it is with the wooden bowl, our views and values placed upon kata practice today differ from those of earlier practitioners.

The precise time that the Okinawan civil fighting arts were first developed is hard to ascertain. Primarily because of the tradition of transmitting history orally, a lack of written records pertaining to the Okinawan fighting arts exists and what records did exist were lost during wartime bombings and the battle for Okinawa during World War II. It is known, however, that systematic methods of hand-to-hand fighting existed on Okinawa as far back as the fourteenth century when the island was originally divided into three separate kingdoms, all at war with each other. By 1429 A.D. the island had been united under one government, but it was not until the sixteenth century that the Okinawan king Sho Shin ended feudalism and prohibited the private ownership of weapons. Unfortunately, peace ended in 1609 when the Satsuma clan from Southern Kyushu invaded and conquered Okinawa. The Japanese once again placed a weapons ban to prohibit any attempts of resisting the occupation. In 1879 A.D. the island was made part of Japan and much of the Okinawan culture came to be directly influenced by the Japanese, including their native fighting arts, which upon being introduced to Japan in the early twentieth century came under the control of the *Dai Nippon Butoku-kai*.

The impetus for the Okinawan civil fighting art's development was due in part to the Satsuma's occupation of the island during which the samurai commonly committed acts of rape, pillage and plunder. At this time, Okinawa had active communication with other cultures through which knowledge of numerous fighting arts came to Okinawa. Through these two forces, and the pre-existing methods of empty-handed fighting present in the Okinawan culture, the foundation was laid for what is known today as karate. The martial knowledge transmitted to the Okinawans from other cultures was often done through kata or pre-arranged training forms. These were then assimilated into the Okinawan fighting arts and in doing so, they began to take on distinctly Okinawan characteristics.

The purpose of each kata used in the Okinawan fighting arts was to preserve and transmit a complete set of techniques and strategies. In writing about *xingyiquan*, Dr. Yang Jwing-Ming said, "Like *taijiquan,* but unlike external styles, *xingyiquan* has only a limited number of practice routines which reflect the depth and profundity of the art's principles. This means that while it is easy to learn *xingyi,* it is hard to comprehend the deeper essence and meaning of the art." (Yang, Liang, *Xingyiquan* 18) Dr. Yang's statement implies that the techniques that make up kata can often become metaphors, which spur on the practitioner to explore other possible uses for them. Likewise, it is not unusual to find one kata that is in itself a complete system that encompasses not only striking methods, but also grappling, throwing, joint locking, strangulation techniques, and even weapons, in addition to empty-handed methods of application. This often proved true for many of the earlier Okinawan kata that were either developed by the Okinawans or were introduced from another country where, in addition, to their numerous combative applications, other areas of development came to be associated with them. In discussing the magnitude of Okinawan karate kata Patrick McCarthy listed the following behavioral traits gained from kata practice in addition to the techniques found.

- *Yoi no kishin* (mental preparation)
- *Inyo* (yin/yang—understanding the magnitude of cause and effect)
- *Go no sen, sen no sen,* and *sen* (three aspects of defensive initiative)
- *Maai* (understanding engagement distance and how to utilize *ma*—the space or interval established through body-change) and *tai sabaki* (expansion and contraction, gyration and body mechanics)
- *Chikara no kyojaku* (the proper amount of power for each technique)
- *Kiai-jutsu* (the gathering and releasing of *ki* or *Qi*)
- *Waza no kankyu* (the speed and rhythm of technique)
- *Ju no ri* (the principle of resiliency and the willingness to bend in the wind of adversity)
- *Bunkai* (understanding the defensive themes and

application of technique)

- *Zanshin* (mental alertness and continued domination before and after the fact)
- *Seishi o choetsu* (transcending the thoughts of life and death)

As McCarthy said about the depths of learning within the Okinawan karate kata, "Through understanding the magnitude of kata, especially when it is combined with spiritual doctrines, it becomes perfectly clear how a single paradigm (kata) can represent an entire fighting art." (McCarthy, *Ancient Okinawan Martial Arts,* 109) Therefore, each kata was considered a complete fighting art within its own right and as such, Okinawan fighters would only practice a handful of the pre-arranged training rituals. They were studied in-depth, which meant that each form was taken apart and examined in minute detail, not in a broad based manner as is seen today. Kata was meant to be perfected and understood in the same manner in which the master woodworker looks at his craft. This took much time, but in doing so a karate-ka could come to understand the entire art of fighting. Okinawan karate great Gichin Funakoshi wrote about the practice of kata during the late nineteenth century that,

> Night after night, often in the backyard of the Azato house as the master looked on, I would practice a kata (formal exercise) time and again week after week, sometimes month after month, until I had mastered it to my teacher's satisfaction. This constant repetition of a single kata was grueling, often exasperation and on occasion humiliating. More than once, I had to lick the dust on the floor of the dojo or in the Azato backyard. But practice was strict, and I was never permitted to move on to another kata until Azato was convinced that I had satisfactorily understood the one I had been working on.
> —(Funakoshi, *Karate-do My Way of Life,* 22)

With the introduction of Okinawan karate to Japan this practice changed; the traditional method of studying was

GICHIN FUNAKOSHI

replaced by one that stressed breadth instead of depth. Karate-ka came to embrace a mindset of more is better and whereas previously only a handful of kata were practiced, this was discarded in favor of collecting kata and practicing them on a more superficial level than was previously done on Okinawa. Kata's role in the new karate-do was viewed not so much as a means to transmit and perfect combative techniques, but instead as tools to train karate-ka in the fundamental movements found within the newly organized karate-do systems. What had once been taught to small and often select groups was now being offered to the masses, but it was done not without protest. Karate great Shoshin Nagamine reflected on this change when he recounted a conversation he once had with the legendary Motobu Choki. Nagamine said about Motobu Choki's comments,

> He was sad that with the popularity of the discipline there also had come great change. The kata practiced in Tokyo had been carelessly changed, and in some cases completely disintegrated. In Okinawa, during the old days, students spent years meticulously learn-

ing a single kata or two. That custom in Tokyo had changed to the pointless but popular practice of accumulating many kata without ever understanding their respective applications. The practice of kata had been reduced to stiff and fixed postures, without tai sabaki (body movement) or ashi sabaki (stepping and sliding) Kata had become a lifeless practice, Motobu believed.

—(Nagamine, *Okinawa Masters*, 100)

The kata had become very standardized routines that were performed and not studied as had been before. They were viewed as a whole entity instead of a group of proven techniques that were to be taken from the kata and studied on an individual basis. However, this mass standardization of Okinawan kata allowed the fighting art of karate to be taught to large groups of people who in turn came to place different values upon kata practice than what were originally found in Okinawa. Even though the traditional kata may or may not have changed in a physical sense, they served a different purpose for the new breed of karate-ka. Kata practice came to be admired for reasons other than what it was originally designed for.

Despite the new emphasis placed on kata training by twentieth century karate-ka, the process of coming to understand and explore several levels of personal experience through the study of a single kata or any other pre-arranged training ritual is possible if time is taken to understand the role played by the esoteric, philosophical and religious nuances found within the form. This is due to the pragmatic nature inherent to traditional kata. Which causes a metaphoric side to be present in their practice. The metaphoric nature of kata embraces many of the cultural mores and values inherent to the society from which a fighting art came, one of which was the esoteric belief system of the pre-modern warrior. Although these are often shunned by modern practitioners or otherwise interpreted in a very aesthetic manner today, for the pre-modern man-of-arms they proved to be as much of a necessity as was his sword and shield.

4-1 ESOTERIC REALMS

Our modern world is interpreted through many things: logic, politics, religion, science, art, technology and even business. However, each one of these means of interpretation is a reflection of our current society and its morals and values. The world in which we live is seen largely through mechanistic and technological viewpoints that have come to influence our myths, religions, and philosophical thought. Unlike the fifteenth century man-of-arms who said his prayers or contemplated the meaning of a *mandala* before entering combat, modern day warriors may seek solace in prayer before battle, but their art of war is often conducted through the computer screen of an attack aircraft or scope of a high-powered rifle. These methods of fighting are different from those used by the samurai, mongol, or viking who fought hand-to-hand, close enough to smell his enemy and feel the warmth of his blood as it spattered forth from the stroke of a sword.

In our society today esoteric beliefs are often shunned because of the influence of Western logic resulting from industrialized and technological ways of thought. Today's logic differs considerably than what it originally entailed when Socrates, Plato, Aristotle and other great minds practiced it in classical Greece. Although our modern logic is one that debunks many ancient superstitions, at the same time it has a tendency to separate man from the human experience instead of helping him to understand it more completely. Our logic often reduces the human experience into equations and figures and leaves no room for the traditional realms of exploring man's humanity through myth, metaphor, poetry, literature, philosophy or even mysticism. Joseph Campbell wrote about the role played by myth in our modern world and how we now view it,

> Whenever the poetry of myth is interpreted as biography, history or science, it is killed. The living images become only remote facts of a distant time or sky. Furthermore, it is never difficult to demonstrate that as science and history mythology is absurd.

> When a civilization begins to reinterpret its mytholo-
> gy in this way a life goes out of it, temples become
> museums, and the link between the two perspectives
> is dissolved. Such blight has certainly descended on
> the Bible and on a great part of the Christian cult.
> —(Campbell, *The Hero with a Thousand Faces,* 249)

Unlike our modern views on religion, mythology, and all things esoteric, past cultures embraced these mediums strongly because they were valuable tools for interpreting and understanding the world in which man lived. For instance, today many smirk at the mention of astrology but at one time it was considered a reliable and accurate means of predicting forthcoming events. It was an art form that was practiced by the Indians, Persians, Egyptians, as well as many other advanced societies where it came to be intertwined with both philosophical and religious schools of thought.

When pre-modern warriors embraced these esoteric realms a great deal of symbolism, which reflected their esoteric beliefs, came to be attached to the weapons, techniques, and the katas man-of-arms used. The sword's cross guard was more than a junction for the blade and hand guard; for many European knights it came to symbolize the cross on which Jesus was crucified. This metaphor gave them both strength and a moral right to wage battle. Likewise, the belief in "Passau art" or the ability to make oneself invisible through the use of incantations and charms was embraced and believed by many during medieval times. For us today, such a way of thought may seem superstitious, but it was a very pragmatic undertaking in earlier times performed not out of aesthetics but instead as a method to protect the warrior during combat. In a day and age where something so simple as a common cold could kill a person, any means available to protect the warrior from harm was taken.

For today's modern day infantryman who looses his leg in combat, as tragic as it is, he still has a relatively good chance of survival with modern medicine. However, for the fifteenth century warrior whose leg was cut off during battle, death was most assured either through loss of blood, shock, infection, or all three combined. Because of such harsh circumstances various esoteric realms were incorporated into the civil and military fighting arts and the kata these systems used during pre-modern times. These esoteric additions to the weapons, kata and prearranged movement patterns were often drawn from the culture's religious belief systems. In the Japanese martial arts there is a degree of Buddhism, in Chinese systems, Daoism, and in Indonesian fighting arts Islamic influences can be found. Though the esoteric elements may or may not have held direct bearing on the physical execution of a technique during combat, they still played a major role in the warrior's mental preparation for combat and by doing so became an integral part of his training and kata. Thus, the physical became balanced with the spiritual and in time, this fostered new ideas and experiences within many fighting arts. Kata and pre-arranged forms training came to be viewed as more than just the execution of technique. Instead, it mirrored both life and death; it aided the warrior in his preparation to face death itself. To shun the notion of dying in battle was most assuredly a path towards certain destruction. It could not be ignored, instead it had to be addressed in a very head on manner that left no doubt in the warrior's mind that one false move was all that was needed for his demise. Tsukahara Bokuden (1490-1571 A.D) who reputedly killed 212 swordsmen in battle and duels, wrote,

> If in his mind the warrior doesn't forget one thing
> death, he'll never find himself caught short
> The lesson the warrior learns in every case Is ultimately, finally the one thing: death
> If the warrior proceeds by casting aside the two things, life and death, nothing at all can best his mind.
> —(Bokuden, *The Sword and the Mind*, 14)

Bokuden's words were reflected in the kata he practiced. They were not separate from his sword skills but instead came from its practice, during which he and his training partner were constantly reminded that for each technique there was also a counter technique. Therefore, every time a cut was executed the realization came that in trying to kill an enemy the swordsman might just as easily be killed himself. Without the physical and combative realms associated with the martial arts, Bokuden's words are only reflections on man's spirituality, but when combined with his fencing and expressed through the practice of kata, his words become an attitude towards life that is expressed physically with very pragmatic overtures.

In western societies, varieties of esoteric rituals were incorporated into the fighting arts and their pre-arranged training rituals, some of which even held influence on a person's daily affairs. Prior to the widespread influx of Christianity, many of these rituals were based upon either tribal or pagan beliefs. However, the use and role played within each society differed because of belief systems, trade, and geography, all of which greatly affected the conduct and practice of war. For horse-based societies such as the Huns and Mongols, their methods of warfare were conducted at long range, and their principle weapons were bow and spear. In these instances, a certain emotional detachment to the execution of war was achieved. The distance at which the equestrian population fought afforded them a safety zone where their enemy was not at arms length. The need for esoteric rituals to protect them was not as strong as it was with warriors who fought primarily on foot and at close range. To their enemies, the horseman killed in a cold and calculated manner that seemed almost without risk and with an emotional detachment that held none of the rituals found among foot soldiers. John Keegan wrote of their detachment and its influence on their way of war, "It was the emotional detachment of the horse warriors, ultimately manifest in their deliberate practice of atrocity, which the settled peoples found so terrifying. It nevertheless rubbed off on them. Of the two characteristics of 'primitive' warfare that persisted well into the development of civilization—tentativeness of encounter and association of ritual and ceremony with combat and its aftermath—the horse peoples had truck with neither." (Keegan, *A History of Warfare,* 213) However, for those people who were not of a nomadic existence, where the horse was owned by only the upper or ruling classes and combat was frequently conducted on foot at close range, esoteric rituals were used and these even came to have impact on day-to-day life. The sword also represented in Germanic tribes the luck of the family and was used as a ruler to measure of a man's promise. Upon taking an oath or making a promise, it was commonplace for a warrior to rest his hand upon his sword implying that should he break his word or fail to fulfill his promise then the weapon would turn on its user.

The European warrior, just as his Asian counterpart, would inscribe mystical symbols and signs upon his sword's blade. These talismans were composed of numerical, astrological, and religious symbols and held various meanings, some of which were designed to bring bad luck to an enemy, others for the sword's bearer to have a long and healthy life, while some signified that the sword was to be used only for justice and to defeat evil. Just as the sword became the "soul of the samurai" it ascended to an equal position for the European man-of-arms who held the long blade in both respect and fear. Below is one such talisman that was designed to "make one beloved also to defeat the ill wishing of all enemies." (Wagner, *Cut and Thrust Weapons*, 75)

1. Mars and Fishes
2. Quadratura and the Crab
3. Radil
4. The Moon
5. Progressive signs
6. Mars and Scales (Ibid, 75)

The blades on which the talismans were inscribed were, in some instances used for hundreds of years and were passed on through the generations. This belief in the power of such esoteric forces did not altogether decrease as time went on; in fact, there is evidence to support the belief that it increased with the introduction of firearms on the battlefield. Because the martial artist could now be killed from long range by a commoner armed with a gun, without even the most remote chance to cross swords with his enemy, the embrace of spells, incantations, and the power of lucky coins became quite common. Eduard Wagner wrote about the legend surrounding the protective powers of Mansfeld thalers,

> The legend about this spread swiftly through the army and the price of these thalers rose—due to the efforts of the middlemen—to ten and twenty times the original price. Faith in this legend was again renewed by the case of a colonel of the Sachsen family, von Lisbau, who, in case of need, had a Mansfeld thaler sewn into his clothes. Twice he was shot and each time the blow was warded off by the thaler. The belief spread that these thalers gave protection not only against cut and thrust wounds, or wounds from gun shots, but also from the danger of falling from a horse.
>
> —(Wagner, *Cut and Thrust Weapons*, 67)

To many in our modern world such beliefs sound simplistic, yet today's soldiers are also superstitious about the dangers inherent in their world, just as their pre-modern counterparts were. Having been a paratrooper myself, I remember well I would not make a parachute jump without one particular knife that I always wore. Did the knife have any special protective powers? Maybe it did, maybe it did not, but I can attest to the fact that of all the 23 parachute jumps that I participated in, not once did my parachute fail. On each jump I wore my trusty knife. Likewise in modern sport-martial arts, I have known of practitioners who have their favorite kata, staff, *sais*, and even *gi* that they always wear or compete with, believing that the kata, weapon, or article of clothing has lucky qualities about it.

In many societies the esoteric realms associated with the fighting arts even went so far as to instill the belief that the warrior could become impervious to pain, undefeatable in combat, and even develop the ability to change shape into animals, plants, and reptiles. During the occupation of Antioch in 1097 A.D., Christian crusaders found themselves besieged and outnumbered by a very large Turkish army. Their supplies were running out and with morale low, an enterprising cleric found what he called "A Holy Lance" which was said to have pierced Jesus in his side. The Crusaders who believed the find to be an omen of their invincibility in turn marched out of Antioch and defeated the Turks even though they were heavily outnumbered.

In the Indonesian combative arts, Hinduism, Islam and Christianity were all blended together giving both pragmatic and mystical elements to *pentjak-silat* and *kuntao*. It was the result of mysticism associated with Islam, Hinduism and ancient animalist religions that many Indonesians embraced the belief that they could assume animal forms and were impervious to both pain and death in combat. However, for the ever pragmatic Dutch, who were of Christian faiths, the mysticism the Indonesians found so appealing was not embraced. They came to focus more on the physical elements present in the Indonesian fighting arts rather than the mystical. Yet in many instances, the same training patterns were used by both the Dutch and Indonesian practitioners. This is also evident if we observe the influence of native African religions on the practice of *capoeira*. Earlier practitioners of the fighting art were often believed to hold the same abilities as their Indonesian counterparts. As Bira Almeida wrote of the esoteric beliefs and legends associated with the system, "Stories about *capoeira* and famous *capoeiristas* of the past allude to skills, knowledge, and power beyond normal comprehension. There were *capoeiras* with *corpo-fechado* (closed bodies), invulnerable to bullets; *capoeiras* who transformed themselves into animals or trees to escape persecution; *capoerias* who disappeared at will in a moment of necessity, fighters undefeated in impossible situations; and healers of extraordinary success." (Almeida, *Capoeira,* 150)

For the Chinese and Japanese, Daoist and Buddhist symbolism came to have a great influence on their techniques, weapons, postures, and kata, although in a somewhat different manner than what is found with *capoeira* beliefs. The Daoist theory of the five elements is found in both Chinese and Japanese fighting arts. It embraces the thought that man's world is composed of five basic elements: earth, fire, metal, wood, and water. Each element has the power to give birth to another element and each of these in turn has the power to destroy the other. For instance, metal can give birth to water but in turn, water can also overcome fire. They are usually illustrated in a star shaped pattern as seen below:

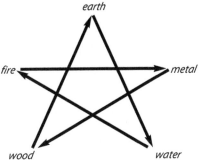

The philosophy of creation and destruction found within the five elements is expressed physically in the fact that there is no superior technique, only the proper movement for the proper time. In the *Koryu bujutsu,* particular elements of this theory are associated with the *kamae* (fighting postures) found within the various *ryu-ha.* Thus, like the elements that are constantly interacting and flowing, the *kamae* themselves are not fixed static postures from which the swordsman never moves, but instead each one flows into the other so that two opponents may assume several different *kamae,* one negating the other before an opening is found.

In *xingyiquan* the five elements correspond to not only particular techniques but also to various organs of the body. Metal corresponds to lungs, water to kidneys, wood to liver, fire to heart, and earth to spleen. These internal organs, the *xingyiquan* practitioner believes, should be developed before one can become a good fighter. In discussing the *Tzuann quan* punching technique, or uppercut as it would be known in western boxing, Master Liang Shou-Yu reflects on the relationship of the five elements to the technique when he wrote, "The motion of *Tzuann*

Quan, although smooth, is fast like thunder. In the theory of the Five Phases, Water is able to grow Wood and conquer Fire. Since *Beng Quan* belongs to Wood and relates to the liver in the Five Phases, *Tzuann Quan* is able to generate *Beng Quan.* For the same reason, *Pau Quan* belongs to Fire and relates to the heart in the Five Phases, and *Tzuann Quan* is able to conquer *Pau Quan.*" (Yang, Liang, *Xingyiquan,* 94) Master Liang's statement reflects the depth of complexity associated with the technique both physically and mentally. The *xingyiquan* practitioner is executing not only a physical movement but also expressing a philosophical idea when his punch is executed. The same occurred with the *Koryu* practitioner, who by assuming a particular *kamae,* expressed not only a martial attitude and intent but also displayed a philosophical way of thought that was injected into the fighting posture by the intersection of esoteric ideas and martial needs.

Just as the poetry and literature of the day, such pre-modern fighting arts embraced a depth in their teachings that touched upon physical, spiritual, philosophical and mental realms. Each posture, technique, and weapon came to symbolize much more than just a mode of attack or defense but instead was a reflection of the culture's mores, attitudes, and philosophical outlook towards life.

The relationship between the esoteric and kata was a bridge between religious and scientific ways of thought. Kata training allows one to physically experience an idea that is wholly philosophical. Zen is not a physical entity, but instead an idea. It is not the word "Zen" that the practitioner seeks to experience but the idea to which the word refers. So to is it with *Qi;* the life force is already present: we have just given it form by expressing it as an idea. Yet the practitioner seeks to experience the idea as a physical reality, therefore, kata becomes a medium that allows them to do so. Kata serves as a vehicle through which an individual can explore and define an idea based purely on philosophical beliefs. Kata came to be far more than just a set of movements linked together and came to be a living, breathing microcosm of the society from which it came that exhibited religious, philosophical, and physical qualities.

4-2 PHYSICAL METAPHORS

As a young karate-ka, I once had a *sensei* who told me that kata was the art of war. For several years I pondered this statement to no avail until I entered the military, and it was there that I began to understand what his words implied. His statement concerns not so much the kata employed on the battlefield, but instead that the use of the kata's techniques were accomplished with a specific strategy in mind. It was within the kata that the strategy could be found, where each technique was executed in a particular manner to allow for timing, distance, and rhythm, all of which were used to create openings in a foe's defense. Likewise, each technique could be used in either a defensive or an offensive mode. These same principles hold true for the infantry squad or rifle platoon, which can be used in an offensive or defensive mode. In the assault, distance and timing has to be taken into account to successfully engage the enemy. Attack too soon and your men will not be ready; attack to late and the enemy will be waiting for you. This applies to the battlefield where successful commanders know how to skillfully deploy and move their troops judging when and where to strike. The same sense of strategy is found in kata, which stresses when and where you should move in relation to an opponent's attack as well as the appropriate timing to use.

This metaphoric relationship between kata and warfare is not new to the annals of the fighting arts but instead has been part of their nature for many years. The same strategies used for war were also used in individual combat. The samurai looked upon his individual duels just as he would battlefield combat. The two were one in the same except that the duel was a microcosmic view of the battlefield's grandiose struggle. The kata he practiced reflected the same attitudes, strategies and techniques; however, the physical realms of kata was a metaphor for much more than just strategy and tactics. They also came to represent the ideas and viewpoints a society embraced concerning health, physical conditioning, spirituality, and even various social issues.

The metaphor was created from and based upon martial reasoning. For instance, the foundation upon which much of the ancient Greeks spirituality rested was the three tenants— strength, beauty, and health, and it was through their Olympic Games and combative sports that these tenants were realized. Winning may have been everything to the Greek boxer but so was a healthy mind and body, and it was through his training that he achieved his trim form and clear mind. As much as his skills and healthy body were admired by others, the value placed upon his athletic prowess was not just from a sense of sportsmanship but also due to the rigors of fighting in the phalanx formation. The classical Greek had to be in prime shape to fight effectively on the battlefield; to be 'unable' would result in not only his own demise but his society's as well. Therefore, the value of a healthy mind and body was one born out of warfare and expressed throughout other mediums in Greek society. The boxer performed his pre-arranged patterns to not only stay in shape and win his match but also to preserve his society's existence.

In terms of physical metaphors, kata and pre-arranged training routines can be viewed with two purposes in mind: combat and conditioning. In this particular instance a combative metaphor does not refer to the particular techniques and weapons used but to the fine art of using them and the where and why of employing a particular strike, cut, or thrust. For instance, the boxer who strikes his opponent on the shoulder with a straight punch will not inflict nearly as much pain as if he had hit his opponent in the solar plexus. Likewise, the duelist whose rapier's thrust punctures a lung has inflicted a very damaging if not lethal blow, whereas the same thrust to his opponent's forearm would not have ended the duel. It was from this lethal process of trial and error, in addition to the birth and practice of various healing arts, that the man-of-arms developed a principle awareness of the body's vital organs, circulatory, and respiratory system. He wanted to be able to kill as efficiently as possible; therefore, he began directing his strikes into those areas that produced the best results. These observations of the cause and effect that certain blows, cuts and thrusts had on the human body greatly impacted the practice of kata and pre-arranged training sequences. The fighter at times set out with a particular strategy in mind: to attack a particular area of his opponent's body with a specific technique designed for the task; however, it was not always the case that the martial artist could easily puncture his foe's most vital organs. When armor was worn the task proved to be much more difficult, and attacks were directed at the armors' weakest points. Some weak points were often covering vital parts of the body; armpits being one such place that armor could not sufficiently protect. A thrust placed here could inflict damage to the nervous and muscular systems, lungs, heart, and even spine depending on its trajectory. Awareness of the vital areas is well known throughout the history of the fighting arts and was incorporated into the practice of combative kata and pre-arranged training routines.

As in language, poetry, and art, the techniques employed in many kata and pre-arranged training sequences came to encompass a depth of combative applications in which the technique itself became a symbolic reminder of their unlimited possibilities. The rapier's thrust could be directed at many areas of an opponent's body, and in every instance the thrusting action was almost the same, even if the technique was directed to a different location. However, each location struck would produce different results: a thrust to the wrist was hardly fatal, yet one to the eye was. Each thrust, though executed in the same manner, came to be a different technique. All were represented by the basic thrusting action practiced by the swordsman. The karate-ka's heel thrust kick can be used against almost any portion of an opponent's body, regardless if they are standing, sitting, or lying down. However, its practice within kata is performed in a consistent manner with the understanding that the technique serves as an example of what can be done with the kick, in addition to illustrating how the kick should be properly executed. This principle of a technique serves as an example of the limitless combative applications found throughout the fighting arts and reflects upon the fluid nature of combat. Static postures are to remind the practitioner of the realms of experience that can be applied to both physical and spiritual natures; the striking of a pose is not done simply for aesthetic purposes.

As with *yin* and *yang*, this lethal awareness also has its non-lethal side. The practice of kata also came to be viewed as a way to enhance one's health, even incorporating elements of a culture's healing arts into its practice. For example, the practice of the *taijiquan* forms opens up the body's energy meridians, exercises its vital organs and stimulates pressure points on the bottom of the feet that contribute to one's health. Aside from its combative applications, the benefits derived from the practice of *taijiquan* are much the same as those gained from *Qigong*, in fact the methods are complementary to one another and at times are merged together during the practice of the *taijiquan* forms. In Okinawan karate the practice of kata, in particular *Sanchin*, has long been associated with health and well-being. *Sanchin*, which uses dynamic tension and deep breathing techniques, is believed to enhance the flow of vital energy throughout one's body, regulate and stimulate internal organs, and even tone and strengthen muscles. For many Okinawan karate-ka, it is believed to contain all areas associated with the practitioner's development both of a physical and spiritual nature. The famed Okinawan karate master Chojun Miyagi stated about the practice of *Sanchin*, "*Sanchin*," Miyagi would say, "should be practiced thirty times a day; in fact, if one were to practice Sanchin all one's life, there would be no reason to learn anything else, Sanchin contains everything." (Bishop, *Okinawan Karate*, 29) Miyagi's observation on the practice of *Sanchin* came to be echoed in other fighting arts and the practice of their pre-arranged training sequences as well.

By the turn of the twentieth century fencing in both Europe and Asia was admired more for its physical attributes than those that once had been combative. For the Japanese or European gentleman who undertook the study of either Kendo or fencing, he did so with the development of spirit and body in mind and not survival on the field of battle. This value adjustment of the fighting arts' kata and pre-arranged training rituals was stimulated by the changing values within many societies. Although the man-of-arms was still needed and still present, he no longer was the entity he once was. With the changing face of warfare from the influx of firearms, combat became a distant affair. It was with the predominant use of firearms that the fighting arts came to be practiced for reasons other than combat. With this evolution, the practice of kata came to be orientated around the alternative reasons and metaphors, instead of a combative rational. Therefore, the study of kata took on new dimensions and assumed new values within modern society that reflected the values of modern man and not those of the pre-modern warrior. While these modern kata are beneficial to the times in which they exist, they often exclude the combative rationale found within traditional kata and pre-arranged training routines. Thus, the warrior ethos and all that it entails comes to be viewed as something apart from the practice of kata instead of an integral part of it.

SANCHIN KATA

CHAPTER 5

Gunpowder and the Classical Warrior's Demise

> When they fired, the smoke came at us in a solid wall.
> Things plucked at my clothes and twitched my hat,
> and when I looked around I saw men all over the
> ground, in the same ugly positions as the men back
> on the slope, moaning and whimpering, clawing at
> the grass. Some were gut-shot, making high yelping
> sounds like a turpentined dog.
>
> —Shelby Foote, *Shiloh*

One of the most interesting figures of the Western martial arts, at least during the nineteenth century, was Sir Richard Burton. An Englishman by birth, Burton lived a life such as one about which novels are written; fluent in many languages, he was an explorer, spy, and writer who published numerous books, one of which is the *Book of the Sword*. Other works include the first English translation of the *Arabian Nights* as well as the *Kama Sutra*. In addition to his numerous intellectual pursuits, Burton was a skilled swordsman who on several occasions had to rely upon his martial prowess in hand-to-hand combat. It was during one of these skirmishes that he was severely wounded by a spear thrust to the face. In his long-standing classic *The Book of the Sword* first published in 1884, Burton wrote about "the queen of weapons" and the Golden Age, which was to him the sixteenth century. "And now arose swordsmanship proper, when the 'Art of Arms' meant, amongst the old masters, the Art of Fence. The sixteenth century was its Golden Age. At this time the Sword was not only the Queen of Weapons, but the weapon paramount between man and man. Then, advancing by slow, stealthy, and stumbling steps, the age of gunpowder, of 'villainous saltpeter,' appeared upon the scene of life." (Burton, *The Book of the Sword,*

xviii) Burton's words reflect upon more than just the transition of one weapon being replaced by another. It speaks about a change in not only the weapons of the day, but the practice of the fighting arts as a whole and with them a reevaluation of the martial artist and his role in society. It also reflects upon the changing social attitudes of the day, for with the ability to kill at a distance, and more importantly the technology to do so on a massive scale, man began to shun the warrior ethos that he once had embraced so strongly. His enemy no longer was an opponent whom he met face to face but instead engaged in a very distant manner far beyond arms length. The symbolism, esoteric reinforcement and mental preparation that once were an integral part of the premodern martial arts were discarded. This was due to not only the distance of engagement at which gun toting armies now fought but also the fact that many of these beliefs came to be shattered by the roar of gunfire. Although pragmatism is a trademark of the successful warrior, for those who came to be so steeply entrenched in esoteric practices, believing that they could withstand the hail of gunfire, the results were often devastating. During the Chinese Boxer Rebellion of 1900, many boxers held the belief that their cultivation of *Qi* would ward off bullets. This esoteric reinforcement, which was based on a naïveté of both firearms and the classical martial arts, resulted in the slaughter of many of their numbers by Westerners armed with bolt action, repeating rifles. The same fate awaited the Filipino Moro who embarked upon a one man Jihad against occupying American forces. The result was death by gunfire instead of the Moro achieving complete victory through his martial and mystical powers, as fierce as they were.

The process of evolution and change brought by the use of firearms was not only found in Europe, but throughout the world. At the battle of Nagashino Japan, in 1575 A.D., 3,000 gunners wrought destruction upon a large force of samurai cavalry, before the horsemen could even close within spears' distance of the gunners' ranks. Their horses shot down under them, chaos reigned in the Takeda army's cavalry as Oda Nobunaga's samurai and foot soldiers finished the slaughter that their arquebuses had begun. Dr. Stephen Turnbull wrote about the battle and its effects on the samurai,: "What therefore is Nagashino's significance? In spite of the Ishiyama Hongan-ji, it remains important as the symbol of a change in military thinking by the daimyo." (Turnbull, *The Samurai,* 77) It was an important change in the samurai's attitude towards warfare; and by the time of Japan's invasion of Korea in 1592 A.D. it was the arquebus that dominated the battlefield and not the katana.

In Europe the use of firearms on the battlefield was initially a love-hate relationship. Many considered guns to be inventions of the devil, far too devastating for use against fellow men. Those who fought with the new weapons were considered cowards and were often executed for doing so. However, the gun's effectiveness could not be overlooked; the bullet's flight made the knight's armor obsolete. In time, attitudes towards the use of firearms and those who used them changed. As it was with the samurai, the gun came to replace the sword as the "Queen of battle" among European men-of-arms. At first the early arquebus were incorporated into the existing infantry formations of the day, alongside pikes, spears, and great swords. Ironically these formations had been devised by military revisionists of the day like Machiavelli and others, who had read the classics by Livy, Josephus, Tacitus, etc. They incorporated the lessons learned by the early Romans and Greeks into Renaissance warfare. These formations and their sense of order brought form and function to both the battlefield and fortifications used by the Renaissance man-of-arms. Thomas Arnold wrote about them and the purpose they served, "Importantly the underlying values at the heart of standard practice—order, pattern, form, precision, repetition—were very similar to the principles disseminated, at the same time and among the same community, by the rules and regulations of angle bastion fortification." (Arnold, *The Renaissance at War,* 66) Thus, once again the principle of kata was applied only on a grander scale and with a new weapon—firearms. The reason for the gun being incorporated into these Renaissance formations was due to the weapon's slow rate of fire that made the gunners easy prey for cavalry once their weapons had been discharged. As its reliability and accuracy increased, the musket, cannon and pistol came to replace those traditional weapons that had dominated warfare for so long. It was the dawning of a new age on the field of battle, one in which the skilled warrior, who had spent most of his entire life training in the martial arts, could be brought down by a commoner, someone untrained in the arts of war save for the ability to pull his musket's trigger on command. Before long, it was the massed ranks of the infantrymen, armed with their muskets who dictated how wars were fought and won instead of the classical warrior who wielded the spear, pike, and sword.

In terms of the fighting arts and their kata, the widespread use of firearms was strongly felt by those who practiced the traditional hand-to-hand based methods. For with the advancement of musketry, a good deal of the classical systems and their pre-arranged training routines slipped by the wayside; many of which were never to be recovered. At first these evolutions on the battlefield helped to advance new systems of civil fighting, for as the musket flourished, so to did the Renaissance martial arts of Europe, particularly those used in the civil sectors. This development was in conjunction with other societies who also had their fighting arts evolve because of similar circumstances. The emergence of the classical *budo* in Japan was the result of the long standing peace of the nation, brought forth due to its unification, which was accomplished in part by the widespread use of firearms on the battlefield. But with the passage of time and changing social attitudes, the civil fighting arts also began to diminish in both their scope and practice. The long-standing traditions of the European fighting guilds faded, and the sword came to be viewed as an instrument used for dueling and sport. Fencing took on an air of competition performed for the development of a sound mind and body instead of surviving the violence that had once been so commonplace. Likewise, with the popularity of *budo* in Japan, the very same weapons that had been used on the battlefield were now implements used to perfect oneself, instead of tools for the waging of war. With their combative rationale diminished, many fighting arts came to be practiced for reasons other than combat and in doing so, their kata reflected these changes. As fencing became a sport in both Europe and Japan, it took on a decidedly sterile nature, in which such techniques as grappling, striking with the sword's hilt, tripping, entrapping, and other such tactics were omitted from the tournament floor. The art of hand-to-hand combat did not completely die out from modern trends, but became obscure within the practice of many modern fighting arts. This proved to be particularly true for those based only upon sport realms where the combative ethos, which was so important in pre-modern combative arts, became unknown with modern day practice.

As man progressed in his ability to wage war, he progressed in other fields, particularly those of communication. In doing so, those traditional methods that he once relied upon to store and transmit knowledge—such as dance, poetry, language and kata—have taken on entirely different roles within modern society. Now the poet, dancer, and warrior are viewed as separate entities and the common link between them goes unrecognized. As technology has spread and influenced the world in which we live, many cultural traditions have been lost. In our society today, the bonds we once held with earlier methods of transmitting and preserving information have been broken and are now maintained by only a small number of people. Likewise, our ability to use the human spirit for transmitting information has been lost and the "epiphany" Joseph Campbell spoke of, is absent in modern transmissions. Thus, the essence of the message often becomes replaced by a one-dimensional sound bite. As the Daoist philosopher Chuang Tzu said, "Words exist because of meaning; once you've gotten the meaning, you can forget the word." *(Chuang Tzu, 140)*

In keeping with this modern trend in both communication and warfare, our bond with kata has also been lost. Today it has become an almost lifeless practice, in which we focus on the "words" Chuang Tzu spoke of and not the meaning. Renowned martial arts author, Donn Draeger, addressed our modern views of both kata and the Asian fighting arts when he said,

> The exponents of today's modern budo gropes about
> in a maze of classical traditions that he does not

understand, and thus, the cleverest of his kind declare that the classical disciplines must be freed from the feudal Japanese superstitions and raised to great heights of rational efficiency so as to yield wealth, prestige, and practical use. Some foreigners proudly declare that they aim to 'Americanize,' or otherwise nationalize Japanese budo in terms more suited to their country's way of life. Most foreigners have self-ish aims that they disguise by mouthing lofty phrases that are nothing but lip service.

—(Draeger, *Modern Budo Bujutsu*, 181)

Both Chuang Tzu's and Mr. Draeger's statements shed much light on our attempts to understand an ancient methodology based on traditions very different from those we value today. Thus, in our attempts to assimilate and re-invent the fighting arts, we often discard the most valuable parts that have proven themselves reliable for many centuries under the harsh extremes of hand-to-hand combat. The rule we use to measure both kata and the classical fighting arts is based on contemporary times and values, not those from which they came. Although the benefits gained by modern man from his practice of kata are numerous (health, well being, physical fitness, etc.) these benefits come not because of the warrior ethos, but rather from their own reasoning; they are not born of a combative rationale. The introspective viewpoint, as well as the spiritual and physical development process so strongly ingrained in combative kata, becomes distilled into one concerned more with winning or losing instead of the duality of life and death that man explored through the mediums of the classical fighting arts' kata.

The world in which we live is one of wealth and comfort, especially when compared to the harsh environments that gave rise to the pre-modern fighting arts. But it is from these differences in time and environments that our misunderstandings of the classical fighting arts originate. This brings about some interesting questions about our modern day practice of the fighting arts and their kata. Can the traditional practice of kata ever be understood in this post modern world of ours? The answer is maybe, but to do so is to study a way that involves much more than a simple bow and the execution of a few crisp movements. To understand a position in the fighting arts is to realize that these training rituals should not be collected but instead explored and experienced in the way a fine wine is appreciated more and more with each sip. The same applies to kata, where each segment should be practiced independently until its deepest realms have been reached and until each technique resonates with a its own distinct flavor.

The purpose of kata training is not to become bound by the form, but to transcend the form itself—to arrive at a point where one can apply its lessons both physically and philosophically. Less means more in the study of kata—more depth of knowledge that is, and this idea runs contrary to how most fighting arts are practiced and taught today. Likewise, for us to fully comprehend kata we need to understand that our present use of the word "traditional" is born of recent times. It reflects neither the long heritage of the classical martial arts, nor the kata that they gave birth to. To study kata as it was intended, is to discard much of what we now embrace and begin afresh by exploring traditions that have long since been laid aside. At best it would prove to be a daunting task but one that if undertaken, would give life and meaning to much more than simply those movements that are performed for the sake of the tournament floor. It should always be remembered that the practice of kata encompasses so much more than just the execution of a few flamboyant routines. At the end of his book *The Fencing Master*, Arturo Perez-Reverte, writes of how the old fencer, Don Jaime, is still searching for the perfect thrust despite his many years of training. "Absorbed in himself, he was trying to remember, fixing in his mind—uninterested in anything else that the universe might contain around him—all the phases that, linked with absolute precision, with mathematical certainty, would lead (he was sure of this now) to the most perfect thrust ever conceived by the human mind." (Perez-Reverte, *The Fencing Master*, 244) For the modern day fighting arts practitioner, Don Jaime's, search for the "perfect thrust" is in essence our search as well. Although many of the fighting arts and kata practiced today are no longer effective in modern day war, it is the development process of both mind and body that they instill from which we benefit. More often than not, our greatest battles will be waged inside of us, and it is on this inner field of battle where we will confront the most formidable enemy of all, ourselves.

Works Consulted

Almeida, Bira. *Capoeria A Brazilian Art Form History, Philosophy, and Practice.* Berkeley: North Atlantic Books, 1986.

Amberger, J Christoph and Pattons Folly. *The Seduction of Art in Military Swordplay.* Hammerterz Forum, Vol.1, No. 1- Summer 1994

_____ *Singlestick, Cudgel Play, and Backswording.* Hammerterz Forum, Vol. 2, No. 3 - Winter 1995/96

_____ *The Dialectics of Death The Warrior Spirit in Ancient Greece.* Hammerterz Forum, Spring/Summer 1996.

_____ *Circumstantial Evidence II The Social Backgrounds of Central European Fencing.* Hammerterz Forum, Vol.1, No. 4-Spring 1995

_____ *Martial Art and Pastime of Fops.* Hammerterz Forum, Volume 1, Number 2 Fall 1994

_____ *Grim Harvest II On the Fatality of Sword-Inflicted Wounds.* Hammerterz Forum Spring Summer 1997 Vol. 3, No.4 & Vol. 4 No. 1

Anglo, Sydney. *The Martial Arts of Renaissance Europe.* New Haven: Yale University Press, 2000.

Armstrong, Hunter B. *Introduction to Hoplology.* Hoplos, Vol. 6, No. 1&2 -Winter 1988

_____ *The Two Faces of Combatives.* International Hoplology Society, Nov 2000

_____ *Pre-Arranged Movement Patterns.* Hoplos, Vol 6, Nos. 1&2-Winter 1988

Armstrong, Karen. *A History of God.* New York: Alfred A. Knopf, 1993.

Arnold, Thomas. *The Renaissance at War.* London: Cassell Publishing, 2001.

Bishop, Mark. *Okinawan Karate Teachers, Styles and Secret Techniques, Second Edition.* Boston: Tuttle Publishing, 1999.

Bradbury, Jim. *The Medieval Archer.* Woodbridge: The Boydell Press, 1985.

Bradford, Ernle. *Termopylae, The Battle For The West.* Da Capo Press, 1993.

_____ *The Sword and The Shield.* London: Penguin Books, 1972.

Brown, Terry. *English Martial Arts.* Norfolk: Anglo-Saxon Books, 1997.

Burton, Richard F. *The Book of the Sword.* New York: Dover Publications Inc, 1987.

Campbell, Joseph. *The Hero with A Thousand Faces.* Princeton: Princeton University Press, 1949.

_____ *The Inner Reaches of Outer Space. Metaphor as Myth and as Religion.* Novato: New World Library, 1986.

_____ *The Power Of Myth with Bill Moyers.* New York: Anchor Books, 1991.

Castiglione, Baldassare. *The Book of the Courtier.* First publication 1561. Translated by Sir Thomas Hoby. Reprint by Everymans Library Dutton: New York 1928

Castle, Egerton. *Schools and Masters of Fencing From the Middle Ages to the Eighteenth Century*. First Publication 1885 by George Bell and Sons. Dover edition published by Dover Publications, Inc Mineola, N.Y. 2003

Ceasar, Julius. *The Gallic Wars*. Translation by John Warrington with preface by John Mason Brown The Heritage Press Norwalk, Connecticut 1955, 1983

Chadwick, Nora. *The Celts, A Lucid and Fascinating History*. London: Penguin Books, 1971.

Chan, Marie. *Chen Shen*. Boston: Twayne Publishers, 1983.

Chuang Tzu. *Basic Writings Translated by Burton Watson*. New York: Columbia University Press, 1964.

Clements, John. *Medieval Swordsmanship*. Boulder: Paladin Press, 1998.

_____ *Renaissance Swordsmanship The Illustrated Use of Rapiers and Cut-and-Thrust Swords*. Boulder: Paladin Press, 1997.

Cohen, Richard. *By The Sword A History of Gladiators, Musketeers, Samurai, Swashbucklers, and Olympic Champions*. New York: Random House, 2002.

De Mente, Boye Lafayette. *The Kata Factor, Japan's Secret Weapon*. Phoenix: Phoenix Books/Publishers, 1990.

DeVries, Kelly. *Infantry Warfare in the Early 14th Century*. Woodbridge, Suffolk UK: Boydell Press 1996.

Diamond, Jared. *Guns, Germs, and Steel*. New York: W.W. Norton & Company, 1999.

Draeger, Donn F. *The Martial-Civil Dichotomy in Asian Combatives*. Hoplos Vol. 3, No1 Feb 1981.

_____ and Gordon Warner. *Japanese Swordsmanship, Technique and Practice*. New York: Weatherhill, 1982.

_____ and Robert W. Smith. *Comprehensive Asian Fighting Arts*. Tokyo: Kodhansha International, 1980.

_____ *Modern Bujutsu & Budo The Martial Arts and Ways of Japan Volume III*. New York: Weatherhill, 1974.

_____ *Classical Bujutsu*. New York: Weatherhill, 1990.

_____ *Classical Budo*. New York: Weatherhill, 1990.

_____ Monograph Series No.2 *Bujutsu and Budo* Edited by Hunter B. Armstrong and Transcribed by Pat Lieberger, Ph.D. Published by the International Hoplology Society 1998

_____ Randori No Kata *AAU/JBBF Judo Handbook* 1966 Edited by Dennis Helm

_____ *Understanding East Asian Combative Culture Part II*. Hoplos- Vol. 7, No. 2 Winter 1992.

Durant, Will. *The Life of Greece*. New York: Simon and Schuster, 1939.

Ebert, James. *A Life in a Year, The American Infantryman in Vietnam, 1965-1972*. Novato: Presidio Press, 1993.

Foote, Shelby. The *Civil War A Narrative Fredericksburg to Meridian*. New York: Vintage Books, A Division of Random House Inc, 1986.

_____ *Shiloh, a Novel*. New York: Vintage Books, A Division of Random House Inc, 1980.

Friday, Karl F. *Legacies of the Sword*. Honolulu: University of Hawaii Press, 1997.

Gala, Matthew S. *The Flower of Battle*. Hammerterz Forum Vol. 2, No. 3 Winter 1995/96

Gibbon, Edward. *The Decline and Fall of the Roman Empire Vol.'s 1-6*. New York: Alfred A. Knopf, 1994.

Goldsworthy, Adrian. *Roman Warfare*. London: Cassell Publishing, 2000.

Grombach, John V. *The Saga of The Fist*. New York: A.S. Barnes and Co., 1949.

Gould, Tony. *Imperial Warriors, Britain and The Gurkhas*. London: Granta Books, 1999.

Graves, Robert. *The Greek Myths*. The Folio Society MCMXCVI London England

Green, Peter. *The Greco-Persian Wars*. Berkley: University of California Press, 1996.

Grossman, Dave. *On Killing The Psychological Cost Of Learning to Kill In War and Society*. Boston: Little, Brown and Co., 1995.

Hall, David A. *Bujutsu And The Esoteric Tradition: Part II of II*. Hoplos November Volume 1, Number 6 1979

_____ *The Yagyu Shinkage Ryu Part 2* Hoplos Winter 1989, Vol. VI, No. 4

Hanson, Victor Davis. *The Wars of the Ancient Greeks*. London: Cassell Publishing, 1999.

_____ *The Western Way of War Infantry Battle in Classical Greece*. New York: Oxford University Press, 1989.

Hargrave, Thomas. *Grappling in Transition: Takeda Sokaku and Kano Jigoro Approaches to Change and Preservation*. Hoplos Winter 1996, Vol., VII, No.4

Hass, Robert. *The Essential Haiku*. Hopewell: The Ecco Press, 1994.

Hayes, Richard. *Hoplology Theoretics An Overview: The Innate/Manifest Imperturbable-Mind/Steadfast-Mind Trait*. Hoplos Fall 1988, Vol. VI, No.3

Heaney, Seamus. *Beowulf, A New Verse Translation*. New York: W.W. Norton & Company, 2000.

Heinrichs, Ann. *Japan Enchantment of the World*. Hong Kong: Grolier Publishing, 1998.

Hohnjec, Primoz. *The Weapons of The Common Folk of Seventeenth Century Carniola According to Valvasor*. Hoplos-Winter 2003, Vol. VIII, No. 1

Homer. *The Iliad translated by Stanley Lombardo*. Cambridge: Hackett Publishing Company Inc., 1997.

Humphreys, Christmas. *A Western Approach to Zen*. Wheaton: The Theosophical Publishing House, 1971.

Hutton, Alfred. *The Sword and the Centuries*. London: Greenhill Books, 2003.

Jansen, Marius. *The Making of Modern Japan.* Cambridge: Harvard University Press, 2000.

Joyner, Tim. *Magellan.* Camden: International Marine, 1992.

Keegan, John. *A History of Warfare.* New York: Vintage Books, 1994.

_____ *The Face of Battle.* New York: Penguin Books, 1978.

Kerr, George H. *Okinawa the History of an Island People.* Boston: Tuttle Publishing, 2000.

Knox, Bernard *The Norton Book of Classical Literature,* New York: Norton 1993

Liang, Shou-Yu & Tai D. Ngo. *Chinese Fast Wrestling for Fighting The Art of San Shou Kuai Jiao.* Boston: YMAA Publication Center, 1997.

Loomis, Roger Sherman and Rudolph Willard. *Medieval English Verse and Prose.* New Jersey: Prentice-Hall Inc., 1948.

Lowry, Dave. *The Classical Japanese Martial Arts in the West: Problems in Transmission.* Koryu.com 10-29-01

_____ *Jo: Art of the Japanese Short Staff.* Santa Clarita: Ohara Publications Inc., 1987.

McCarthy, Patrick. *Ancient Okinawan Martial Arts Koryu Uchinadi Volume 2.* Boston: Tuttle Publishing, 1999.

Machiavelli, Niccolo. *The Prince Translated by W.K. Marriott.* New York: Alfred A. Knopf, 1908.

Manchester, William. *A Word Lit Only By Fire. The Medieval Mind and the Renaissance Portrait Of An Age.* Boston: Little, Brown and Co., 1992.

Marshall, William H. *The Major English Romantic Poets.* New York: Washington Square Press, Inc., 1966.

Mol, Serge. *Classical Fighting Arts of Japan A Complete Guide to Koryu Jujutsu.* Tokyo: Kodansha International, 2001.

Musashi, Miyamoto. *A Book Of Five Rings.* Translated by Victor Harris. Woodstock: The Overlook Press, 1974.

Nardo, Don. *The Ancient Greeks.* San Diego: Lucent Books, 2001.

Niccolle, David. *Medieval Warfare Source Book.* London: Brockhampton Press, 1995.

Newark, Tim. *Warlords Ancient-Celtic—Medieval.* London: Brockhampton Press, England, 1996.

Oakeshott, R. Ewart. *The Archaeology of Weapons Arms and Armour from Prehistory to the Age of Chivalry.* Mineola: Dover Publications Inc., 1996.

Orlando, Bob. *Indonesian Fighting Fundamentals The Brutal Arts of the Archipelago.* Boulder: Paladin Press, 1996.

Ouaknin, Marc-Alain. *Mysteries of the Alphabet.* New York: Abbeville Press Publishers, 1999.

Oxford Dictionary of World Religions. Edited by John Bowker. Oxford University Press Oxford and New York 1997

Palsson, Hermann and Edwards Paul. *Egils Saga* Penguin Translated Edition 1976 Penguin Books London England.

Perez-Reverte, Arturo. *The Fencing Master*. Translated from the Spanish by Margaret Full Costa. A Harvest Book Harcourt, Inc. San Diego New York London. 1988 English Translation 1998

Plato. *The Collected Dialogues*, edited by Edith Hamilton and Huntington Cairns, Princeton University Press, 1961

Poliakoff, Michael B. *Combat Sports In The Ancient World*. New Haven: Yale University Press, 1987.

Pollington, Stephen. *The English Warrior from Earliest Times Till 1066*. Norfolk: Anglo-Saxon Books, 2002.

Pressfield, Steven. *Gates of Fire*. NewYork: Doubleday Books, 1998.

Russell, Bertrand. *The History of Western Philosophy*. New York: Simon and Schuster, 1945.

Russell, Frederick H. *The Just War in The Middle Ages*. London: Cambridge University Press, 1975.

Sinclaire, Clive. *Samurai The Weapons and Spirit of the Japanese Warrior*. Guilford: Lyons Press, 2001.

Skoss, Diane. *Koryu Bujutsu Classical Warrior Traditions of Japan*. Berkeley Heights: Koryu Books, 1997.

_____ Keiko Shokon *Classical Warrior Traditions of Japan Volume 3*. Berkeley Heights: Koryu Books, 2002.

Smith, Robert. *Martial Musings A Portrayal of Martial Arts in the 20th Century*. Erie: Via Media Publishing Company, 1999.

Snodgrass, A.M. *Arms & Armor of the Greeks*. Baltimore: The Johns Hopkins University Press, 1999.

Suzuki, Daisetz T. *Zen and Japanese Culture*. New York: MJF Books, 1959.

Thucydides, *History of the Peloponnesian War*. Translated by Rex Warner. Penguin Books London England 1954

Thurman, Robert. *Inner Revolution, Life, Liberty, and the Pursuit of Real Happiness*. New York: Riverhead Books, 1998.

Turnbull, S.R. *The Samurai A Military History*. New York: Macmillan Publishing Co. Inc., 1977

_____ *Samurai Warfare*. London: Cassell Publishing Wellington House, 1996.

Wagner, Eduard. *Cut and Thrust Weapons*. London: Hamlyn Publishing Group, 1967.

Warry, John. *Warfare in the Classical World*. Norman: University of Oklahoma Press, 1995.

Wiley, Mark. *Filipino Fighting Arts: Theory and Practise*. Burbank: Unique Publications, 2001.

Winters, Yvor. *Forms of Discovery*. Denver: Alan Swallow Press, 1967.

Wrenn, C.L. *A Study of Old English Literature*. New York: W.W. Norton & Company Inc., 1967.

Xenophon. *The March up Country a translation of Xenophon's Anabasis.* Ann Arbor: The University of Michigan Press, 1958.

Yagu, Munenori, Hyoho kadensho, *The Sword and The Mind translated by Hiroaki Sato.* Woodstock: The Overlook Press, 1985.

Yang, Jwing-Ming. *Ancient Chinese Weapons.* Jamaica Plain: YMAA Publication Center, 1999.

_____ and Liang, Shou-Yu and Wu, Wen-Ching. *Baguazhang Theory and Applications.* Jamaica Plain: YMAA Publication Center, 1994.

_____ and Liang, Shou-Yu. *Xingyiquan.* Boston: YMAA Publication Center, 2002.

Yasuda, Kenneth. *The Japanese Haiku.* Tokyo: Charles E. Tuttle Company, 1957.

Zarrilli, Phillip B. *When the Body Becomes All Eyes: Kalarippayattu A South Indian Martial Art.* New Delhi: Oxford University Press, 1998.

End Notes

i. The same can be said about the ancient Germanic tribes of Europe. On the battlefield they were a vicious and brave band of warriors who often fought without body armor, semi-naked, against highly trained, well equipped and armored Roman legions. One particular martial tradition of the Germanic tribesmen was to let their hair and beards grow to extreme lengths, not to be cut until they had killed their first enemy. After doing so, they were considered worthy enough for their faces to be seen by their parents and fellow tribesmen and often was the time when the tribesman would kill his foe and immediately afterwards with the same knife or sword cut his own hair. In the year 9 A.D. the Roman Governor Varus and 15,000 Legionaries were slaughtered in the Teutoburgian forest of Germany by tribesmen of the region. Howling like banshees, the German warriors emerged from the dense undergrowth, using spears, axes, and clubs. The Romans, caught unaware, were unable to maintain cohesive formations and the fighting became man to man. The battle lasted four days, during which time most of the 15,000 Romans were killed. Those taken prisoner were executed; their heads cut off and nailed to trees as further warning for Rome to stay out of German land. Although the Germanic tribesmen did not have the same systematic measure about their fighting arts as did the Romans they still were a society of warriors and embraced a martial ethos, which ran throughout their society. The measure of systematization used by a culture to define its fighting arts varies and a highly stylized method of fighting does not always mean victory, as is the case and point here.

ii. Although these time frames are subject to the individual's own interpretation, some may place the end of the primitive era at the time of Homer's Iliad while others may consider it around 1,000 B.C. In describing theses eras it is much the same as describing when the Middle Ages of Europe ended and the Renaissance began. There is no clear cut off, each era meshed into the other.

iii. The definition of pre-modern and modern fighting arts is based on the use of firearms, however, it is not one that can always be applied to all cultures and societies. It is a case by case study, and in some instances where populations were small and the areas remote, pre-modern methods of fighting were used up until the twentieth century. The native tribes of New Guinea are one such example. The rugged terrain of New Guinea and its reasonably small population, many who live in remote areas, primitive methods of warfare and farming still exist to this very day.

iv. The long standing belief that all martial arts originated around 525 A.D. when Da Mo traveled from India to China, after which they were then transmitted to all points of the globe is not accurate. Just as language, poetry, the written word and the development and use of weapons evolved in many different locations and societies around the world, the same holds true for the evolution and development of mans fighting arts. Their existence if credited to any one reason would be warfare, but it cannot be attributed to the efforts of any one individual no matter how great their contributions may be.

v. "Enlistment was for twenty years; equipment was uniform; and pay was raised by Cease from 120 denarii to 225 denarii a year, less a deduction for rations." (Ceasar *The Gallic Wars*, xxv)

vi. Despite the fact that occupants of the chariot were armed, its weight alone would be enough to kill a man due to the heavy bronze armor of both the vehicle and its passengers.

vii. To quote Victor Davis Hanson who said about this era in Greek History, "And while archaeologists often talk of a 'catastrophe' that brought on the destruction of an entire culture, from a strictly military standpoint the sudden end to a collective autocracy changed forever the direction of Greek warfare. For the first time, the very space, time, equipment and purpose of warfare passed from the autocrat in the citadel to the hands of the individual, in a manner previously unseen in the Mediterranean." (Hanson, *The Wars of the Ancient Greeks,* 33)

viii. For the contemporary practitioner to get an idea of how difficult this is, take a back pack and place a 50 pound dumbbell in it and then walk at a fast pace around your block. Even if you are in shape, the experience will leave you winded and is nothing compared to fighting full contact wearing the backpack and an additional 20 extra pounds put in it.

ix. In Plato's *Laws* the Athenian said about wrestling and its use on the battlefield that, "To come to wrestling, the devices introduced into their systems by Antaeus or Cercyon-or again into boxing by Epeus or Amycus-from mere idle vainglory, are useless in encounters in the field and unworthy of celebration. But anything which comes under 'stand-up wrestling,' can be practiced with spirit and gallant bearing to the benefit of strength and health, is serviceable for all occasions and may not be neglected." (Plato, *Collected Dialogues,* Laws VII 796 A P. 1368)

x. "It was Aristotle who coined the term "just war," applying it to wars waged by Hellenes against non-Hellenes whom he considered barbarians." (Russell, *The Just War in The Middle Ages,* 3-4)

xi. This tactic is one not known to just the Greeks, in fact it has been used by many individuals and armies throughout the history of warfare. In A Book Of Five Rings Miyamoto Musashi describes this very same tactic when he wrote; "When the enemy attacks, remain undisturbed but feign weakness. As the enemy reaches you, suddenly move away indicating that you intend to jump aside, then dash in attacking strongly as soon as you see the enemy relax.(Musashi, *A Book of Five Rings,* 72)

xii. David A. Hall who holds Ph.D.'s in both Buddhist studies and Military History wrote about Marishiten that, "Marishiten's popularity among Japanese warriors was primarily due to the particular synergy of combative powers with which the goddess was thought to empower her devotees: invisibility, the ability to confuse enemies, clarity of mind, intuition, imperturbability, selflessness and, ultimately, compassion." (Hall, *Koryu Bujutsu* 89)

xiii. Although Zen and its exploration of the psyche is thought of as something unique to only Asian cultures, similar disciplines and experiences can also be found in western traditions. Jewish, Islamic and Christian mysticism all explore the human psyche, on a level just as profound as that found within Zen teachings. In describing their exploration of the psyche Jewish Mystics explained it as the journey to God's Throne through the seven heavens and it was said that during the process they flew to the Throne of God. It was only in imagination however that they flew, and the journey itself was symbolic of the exploration of their own mind. Often the assumption is made when discussing the western traditions that no such elements as satori existed but this can be a miss-interpretation. Just because western martial artists did not use the term "zen" does not mean that the same focus of mind was not found within their martial arts. In Castiglone's 1561 publication, *The Book Of The Courtier,* he writes of the mindset a swordsman should have when entering combat. "Neither let him runne rashly to these combats, but when he must needes to save his estimation withall: for beside the great daunger that is in the doubtful lot, he that goeth headlone to these thinges, and without urgent cause, deserveth great blame, although his chaunce bee good." (Castiglione, *The Book of the Courtier*, 40)

xiv. The Japanese, and Asian fighting arts as a whole, were not the only cultures to utilize organized systems of teaching and transmitting, techniques and tactics. This was also done in European martial arts with the London Masters of Defense and other European Fencing guilds of the day. Due to the violence so prevalent of the times, during the middle ages and renaissance period there was often a love/hate relationship towards these European martial artists. However this did not prevent schools of arms, which had professional teachers, to be organized with royal blessings. As with the Japanese *ryu-ha*, the European schools of arms teachings also encompassed swords, pole-arms, knife, and empty-handed methods of combat. Henry the VIII was one royal who condoned and supported the establishment of the London masters of defense. Likewise throughout the rest of Europe, fighting guilds became established which had systematic methods of teaching and strict ranking systems. Often various regions were noted for having guilds associated with them, whose teachings were recognized as being the "official school or style" of that area. The European schools though, unlike the Japanese bujutsu, which were practiced only by the samurai, did allow and even encouraged citizens to partake in their training. Two of the most well known and respected fighting arts guilds in Europe during the sixteenth century were the Marxbruder and Federfechter schools whose ranks were filled with craftsmen.

xv. Mantras are instruments of thought expressed through verses or syllables that hold divine power, and are used in both Buddhism and Hinduism. (Oxford Dictionary of World Religions, 615) Mudras are physical signs that express a spiritual reality and are often performed with the hands, and often accompany a Mantra

xvi. The professional warrior's role became lost in the industrial age. With the advent of firearms his position became threatened due to the fact that it became far easier to train a musketeer to do in 5 months time what took a skilled man-of-arms to learn how to do with sword, pole arm, bow and arrow in as much as three to five years. The musketeer's weapons became far more deadly than those used by the swordsman, especially as firearms technology advanced. With the coming of the industrial age, machines and industrialized thinking came to the battlefield making it far more deadly and impersonal than ever before. The individuality once so important to the man-of-arms became replaced by the industrialized mindset that stressed conformity instead of individuality. With the advent of tanks, airplanes, battleships, flamethrowers and landmines, man is able to kill in a very orderly almost production like manner that often distanced him from his enemy. To attempt combat man to man on the modern battlefield would almost surely amount to suicide for both parties involved. The way of the warrior came to be replaced not only in actions but in thought and spirit as well.

xvii. This also proves true for transmission of information about fighting arts. Much of this has been done by oral transmission through, songs, poems and folklore, in both European and Asian societies. It has also led to gaps as to when, where, and how various styles and systems developed. The Okinawan fighting arts are one such example. Much of their history was passed on by oral transmission and was lost over time. This was compounded by the fact that many written records were lost during World War II due to the numerous bombings the island suffered, not to mention the devastation wrought on its civilization from the battle that raged on the Island in 1945. In terms of Chinese martial arts, historical novels written during the course of Chinese history do shed some light upon the systems and their evolution however they are not all conclusive and do not encompass all of the vast history of China.

xviii. St. Augustine's Just war precept is even reflected in modern literature. In Arturo Perez-Reverte's *The Fencing Master* the conversation between Don Jaime and Romero serves as an example of Augustine's views when Romero states that he is against all violence, Don Jaime replies: "Well, I'm not. There are very subtle shades of violence, I can assure you. A civilization that renounces the possibility of resorting to violence in thought or deed destroys itself. It becomes a flock of sheep that will get their throats cut by the first person to come along. The same thing happens to men." (Perez-Reverte, *The Fencing Master,* 119) It is not that Don Jamie is for the unrestricted use of violence but instead that he understands that at certain times it is justified to use force in order to protect ones self or the lives of others, including the protection of ones country.

xix. Cohen p. 57 By the Sword

xx. One of the more famous women-of-arms to benefit from dance was Helene Mayer, a German girl who, in 1928, captured the Olympic Gold medal in fencing. She was an excellent athlete skilled in riding, swimming, skiing, ballet, and fencing. Born in 1910 she continued her ballet training until the age of 13 when she began to study fencing. Her skills were soon noted throughout Europe as she competed and won many events, often against men.

xxi. When the Okinawan Fighting arts were introduced to Japan, they came under the regulation of the *Di Nippon Butoku-kai* or Great Japan Martial Virtues Association Martial Arts Specialty School, which was a militaristic organization organized in 1911 and tasked with the job of embedding a martial spirit into the Japanese society. One of the ways this was accomplished was through the mandatory practice of modern budo systems, such as Judo and Kendo. In as such, the Okinawan fighting arts were used in the same manner as the Japanese budo were. This also entailed a standardization of kata, formalized ranks and uniforms, and the injection of a militaristic philosophy into the Okinawan systems, one, which had previously not existed. In the words of Patrick McCarthy, the Japanese looked upon the Okinawan fighting arts: "This, together with the disorganized teaching curricula, lack of social decorum, and absence of formal practice apparel, testing standards, and competitive element, compelled the Butoku-kai to regard the situation as detrimental to Todui-jutsu's growth and direction within the mainland, and set forth to resolve it." (McCarthy, *Ancient Okinawan Martial Arts,* 82) Prior to this, the Okinawan fighting arts were segmented more so by region and teacher than by *ryu-ha* or style. Thus, in implementing their changes, the Japanese made Okinawan Karate more accessible to the masses and at the same time generic in its presentation.

xxii. In Japan, the practice of kata is applied to almost everything within their culture. The term Shikata literally translates into "the way of doing things" and is used as a means of organization, practice, and training, throughout their society; in dance, poetry, art, tea ceremonies, reading, as well as their martial arts, kata is used. Boye Lafayette De Mente said of the role kata plays in Japanese society that: "When used in the Japanese context the shikata concept includes more than just the mechanical process of doing something. It also incorporates the physical and spiritual laws of the cosmos. It refers to the way things are supposed to be done, both the form and the order, as a means of expressing and maintaining harmony in society and the universe." (De Mente, *The Kata Factor,* 13) The same held true within western societies where there was a proper way and ritualized method of performing religious ceremonies, marriages, duels, writing, reading and even conducting warfare.

xxiii. This is not to say that all kata are alike, for they are not. But there are physical similarities to be found within many. It is often the case that what distinguishes the technique is not its physical movement but the intent behind it. In using the analogy of a Japanese martial art verses martial way, the samurai who executed a downward cut on the battlefield did so with the intent to kill his foe. However for the twentieth century Kendo player the same movement executed in competition is done not to kill, but to score a point on his opponent.

xxiv. Magellan's battle was for one of the oldest reason known to man, infidelity. After encountering the men of Cebu, the explorers noted two things in particular about them, one, that they were allowed to have as many wives as they wanted, the other, that their penises were pierced from side to side with a gold bolt. This made intercourse with their wives very painful. The women upon encountering Magellan's men became aware of the difference between them and their husbands. As Tim Joyner wrote, "It is easy to understand why the women of Cebu preferred Magellan's sailors to their husbands and usual lovers, and Magellan's men were more than willing to oblige them." (Joyner, *Magellan,* 190) This led to unrest amongst the Cebu men and a refusal to submit to Magellan's authority, in particular one tribal chieftain by the name of Lapulapu. Upon learning this, Magellan set out with only 60 men to enforce his rule upon the Cebu Chief and make an example of him in the process. Things did not turn out as Magellan had wished, he encountered a strong force of well armed Filipino warriors who killed and wounded several of his men before they could retreat back to their boats. For Magellan however it was his last battle.

xxv. The reluctance to engage the enemy in hand-to-hand combat is strong even in today's military. In discussing the amount of ammunition he carried in a combat zone Vietnam Veteran Terry Shepardson said, "There was no way I was going to get caught without ammunition. I paid the consequences because I grunted and was tired every day from marching, but I never ran out of ammo. Matter of fact, I'd always have a few rounds to spare. There was no way I was going to go hand-to-hand with nobody. No way! I wanted plenty of rounds with me. I had a fear: some gook running at me with a three-foot blade, sticking me in the guts because I didn't have any ammo. I didn't want that." (Elbert, *A Life in a Year,* 162) In discussing the fighting arts many forget that the development of weapons were one of man's first priorities. Hand-to-hand combat, especially unarmed, is considered a worst case scenario; from pre-historic man to the present day, with all the physical and psychological factors involved.

Index

BOOKS FROM YMAA

DVDS FROM YMAA

ADVANCED PRACTICAL CHIN NA IN-DEPTH
ANALYSIS OF SHAOLIN CHIN NA
ATTACK THE ATTACK
BAGUA FOR BEGINNERS 1
BAGUA FOR BEGINNERS 2
BAGUAZHANG: EMEI BAGUAZHANG
BEGINNER QIGONG FOR WOMEN 1
BEGINNER QIGONG FOR WOMEN 2
BEGINNER TAI CHI FOR HEALTH
CHEN STYLE TAIJIQUAN
CHEN TAI CHI FOR BEGINNERS
CHIN NA IN-DEPTH COURSES 1—4
CHIN NA IN-DEPTH COURSES 5—8
CHIN NA IN-DEPTH COURSES 9—12
FACING VIOLENCE: 7 THINGS A MARTIAL ARTIST MUST KNOW
FIVE ANIMAL SPORTS
FIVE ELEMENTS ENERGY BALANCE
INFIGHTING
INTRODUCTION TO QI GONG FOR BEGINNERS
JOINT LOCKS
KNIFE DEFENSE: TRADITIONAL TECHNIQUES AGAINST A
    DAGGER
KUNG FU BODY CONDITIONING 1
KUNG FU BODY CONDITIONING 2
KUNG FU FOR KIDS
KUNG FU FOR TEENS
LOGIC OF VIOLENCE
MERIDIAN QIGONG
NEIGONG FOR MARTIAL ARTS
NORTHERN SHAOLIN SWORD : SAN CAI JIAN, KUN WU JIAN,
    QI MEN JIAN
QI GONG 30-DAY CHALLENGE
QI GONG FOR ANXIETY
QI GONG FOR ARMS, WRISTS, AND HANDS
QIGONG FOR BEGINNERS: FRAGRANCE
QI GONG FOR BETTER BREATHING
QI GONG FOR CANCER
QI GONG FOR ENERGY AND VITALITY
QI GONG FOR HEADACHES
QI GONG FOR HEALING
QI GONG FOR HEALTHY JOINTS
QI GONG FOR HIGH BLOOD PRESSURE
QIGONG FOR LONGEVITY
QI GONG FOR STRONG BONES
QI GONG FOR THE UPPER BACK AND NECK
QIGONG FOR WOMEN
QIGONG FOR WOMEN WITH DAISY LEE
QIGONG MASSAGE
QIGONG MINDFULNESS IN MOTION
QIGONG: 15 MINUTES TO HEALTH
SABER FUNDAMENTAL TRAINING
SAI TRAINING AND SEQUENCES
SANCHIN KATA: TRADITIONAL TRAINING FOR KARATE POWER
SCALING FORCE
SHAOLIN KUNG FU FUNDAMENTAL TRAINING: COURSES 1 & 2
SHAOLIN LONG FIST KUNG FU: ADVANCED SEQUENCES 1
SHAOLIN LONG FIST KUNG FU: ADVANCED SEQUENCES 2
SHAOLIN LONG FIST KUNG FU: BASIC SEQUENCES
SHAOLIN LONG FIST KUNG FU: INTERMEDIATE SEQUENCES
SHAOLIN SABER: BASIC SEQUENCES
SHAOLIN STAFF: BASIC SEQUENCES
SHAOLIN WHITE CRANE GONG FU BASIC TRAINING: COURSES
    1 & 2

SHAOLIN WHITE CRANE GONG FU BASIC TRAINING: COURSES
    3 & 4
SHUAI JIAO: KUNG FU WRESTLING
SIMPLE QIGONG EXERCISES FOR HEALTH
SIMPLE QIGONG EXERCISES FOR ARTHRITIS RELIEF
SIMPLE QIGONG EXERCISES FOR BACK PAIN RELIEF
SIMPLIFIED TAI CHI CHUAN: 24 & 48 POSTURES
SIMPLIFIED TAI CHI FOR BEGINNERS 48
SUNRISE TAI CHI
SUNSET TAI CHI
SWORD: FUNDAMENTAL TRAINING
TAEKWONDO KORYO POOMSAE
TAI CHI BALL QIGONG: COURSES 1 & 2
TAI CHI BALL QIGONG: COURSES 3 & 4
TAI CHI BALL WORKOUT FOR BEGINNERS
TAI CHI CHUAN CLASSICAL YANG STYLE
TAI CHI CONNECTIONS
TAI CHI ENERGY PATTERNS
TAI CHI FIGHTING SET
TAI CHI FIT: 24 FORM
TAI CHI FIT: FLOW
TAI CHI FIT: FUSION BAMBOO
TAI CHI FIT: FUSION FIRE
TAI CHI FIT: FUSION IRON
TAI CHI FIT: HEART HEALTH WORKOUT
TAI CHI FIT IN PARADISE
TAI CHI FIT: OVER 50
TAI CHI FIT OVER 50: BALANCE EXERCISES
TAI CHI FIT OVER 50: SEATED WORKOUT
TAI CHI FIT OVER 60: GENTLE EXERCISES
TAI CHI FIT OVER 60: HEALTHY JOINTS
TAI CHI FIT OVER 60: LIVE LONGER
TAI CHI FIT: STRENGTH
TAI CHI FIT: TO GO
TAI CHI FOR WOMEN
TAI CHI FUSION: FIRE
TAI CHI QIGONG
TAI CHI PUSHING HANDS: COURSES 1 & 2
TAI CHI PUSHING HANDS: COURSES 3 & 4
TAI CHI SWORD: CLASSICAL YANG STYLE
TAI CHI SWORD FOR BEGINNERS
TAI CHI SYMBOL: YIN YANG STICKING HANDS
TAIJI & SHAOLIN STAFF: FUNDAMENTAL TRAINING
TAIJI CHIN NA IN-DEPTH
TAIJI 37 POSTURES MARTIAL APPLICATIONS
TAIJI SABER CLASSICAL YANG STYLE
TAIJI WRESTLING
TRAINING FOR SUDDEN VIOLENCE
UNDERSTANDING QIGONG 1: WHAT IS QI? • HUMAN QI
    CIRCULATORY SYSTEM
UNDERSTANDING QIGONG 2: KEY POINTS • QIGONG
    BREATHING
UNDERSTANDING QIGONG 3: EMBRYONIC BREATHING
UNDERSTANDING QIGONG 4: FOUR SEASONS QIGONG
UNDERSTANDING QIGONG 5: SMALL CIRCULATION
UNDERSTANDING QIGONG 6: MARTIAL QIGONG BREATHING
WATER STYLE FOR BEGINNERS
WHITE CRANE HARD & SOFT QIGONG
YANG TAI CHI FOR BEGINNERSS
WUDANG KUNG FU: FUNDAMENTAL TRAINING
WUDANG SWORD
WUDANG TAIJIQUAN
XINGYIQUAN

more products available from . . .

YMAA Publication Center, Inc. 楊氏東方文化出版中心

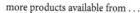

1-800-669-8892 • info@ymaa.com • www.ymaa.com